A Guide and Handbook for Those Who Care About Creating and Supporting **Quality in Schools**

# L    g
# Learning
# Communities

**SECOND EDITION**

UPDATED AND EXPANDED

Standards for What

## Principals

Should

## Know

and Be Able

## To Do

National Association of Elementary School **Principals**

**naesp**

*Leading Learning Communities: Standards for What Principals Should Know and Be Able To Do* was created by the National Association of Elementary School Principals in partnership with Collaborative Communications Group.

---

**National Association of Elementary School Principals**
1615 Duke Street
Alexandria, VA 22314
Phone: 800-38-NAESP
Fax: 800-39-NAESP
E-mail: naesp@naesp.org
Web site: www.naesp.org

The mission of the National Association of Elementary School Principals (NAESP) is to lead in the advocacy and support for elementary and middle level principals and other education leaders in their commitment to all children. Over 30,000 members of NAESP provide administrative and instructional leadership for public and private elementary and middle schools throughout the United States, Canada and overseas. Founded in 1921, NAESP is an independent professional association with its own headquarters building in Alexandria, Virginia. Through national and regional meetings, award-winning publications and joint efforts with its 50 state affiliates, NAESP is a strong advocate for both its members and for the 33 million American children enrolled in preschool, kindergarten and grades 1 through 8.

Gail Connelly, Executive Director
Fred Brown, Senior Associate Executive Director, Leadership Development and Outreach
Merrie Hahn, Assistant Executive Director, Professional Development Programs

---

**Collaborative Communications Group, Inc.**
1029 Vermont Avenue, NW
Ninth Floor
Washington, D.C. 20005
Phone: 202-986-4959
Fax: 202-986-4958
E-mail: info@collaborativecommunications.com
Web site: www.collaborativecommunications.com

COLLAB⊙RATIVE
COMMUNICATIONS GROUP

Collaborative Communications Group is a strategic consulting firm that builds the capacity of individuals, organizations and networks to work collaboratively to create solutions that are better than any single entity could produce on its own. Through strategic consulting, dialogue and convening, creation of publications and tools, and community conversations, Collaborative helps organizations and networks to identify, share and apply what they know in ways that increase productivity and effectiveness. The ultimate objective of Collaborative's work is the improvement of the quality of public education and community life.

---

Funds for this publication were generously donated by **Lifetouch Inc.**, of Minneapolis, MN, Paul Harmel, Chairman and Chief Executive Officer. Lifetouch Inc. connects with families and communities, not only in the images it captures, but also in its support of many worthwhile causes.

---

Funds for this publication were generously donated by **Landscape Structures**, of Delano, MN. Since 1971, Landscape Structures, the industry's leading provider of high-quality school playground equipment, has been committed to promoting sustainable communities, healthier kids and a healthier planet.

# Table of Contents

# Foreword

**Gail Connelly, Executive Director**

I n an age of heightened accountability, it is particularly important to remember that creating and sustaining good schools is about more than academic performance. That's why NAESP remains focused on the culture of how principals lead and work in a learning community. In this document, we give language to our values and beliefs about the elements of that learning culture in schools.

We intentionally do more in this publication than simply describe the state of principal practice as it exists. Instead, we define what learning, places of learning and learning communities can be. We know that all schools strive to perform at the highest levels possible, but realize that for some principals and schools, the ultimate leadership continuums described here may be daunting, yet hopefully aspirational. But by giving language and images to effective learning communities, we believe that we can help principals define their desired practice and thus take important steps in achieving their aspirations.

We have also intentionally focused on the interpersonal aspect of a principal's role, responding to what most effective leaders already know: It's the quality and collective purpose of collaborative relationships that can transform a group of people working together into a true learning community.

In this updated edition of *Leading Learning Communities*, along with various initiatives under way at NAESP, we face squarely the challenges inherent in the transformation of our global society. While we might have seen glimpses of the future for learning and for leaders in the recent past, global transformation is now a stark reality for everyone.

This new reality requires even more attention to drawing connections across languages and sectors—particularly in the need to create new approaches to learning that bridge schools and communities. With an increasing diversity of ethnicities, languages, learning needs and perspectives in our communities, a principal's cultural competence is more important than ever.

As we embrace the changes in education and society, our sense of personal and professional accountability is heightened. All of the content in this publication is linked to accountability for better performance of students as well as adults. Throughout the publication, we address the growing need not just to collect data but also to sort, filter and use it to improve learning and growth.

At the same time, we know that accountability goes beyond test scores. In addition to helping children be intellectually active, we must also be accountable for helping them be physically, verbally and socially engaged. Educated children must be academically proficient. And, in an increasingly diverse and global society, educated children must also be creative, curious and imaginative. NAESP supports efforts to help children become strong students and critical thinkers, confident, cared for and valued.

We have set the bar high: We know that living up to the standards in this document will require a serious commitment and an intense individual and collective effort. We also know that principals will need support and resources on their journey toward mastery. So in addition to painting a picture of what high-performing school learning communities look like, NAESP has defined strategies that provide a roadmap of how to create and sustain them. We urge all principals to embrace these high standards and engage their learning communities toward assuring all children reach their highest potential.

In this updated and expanded edition, we look specifically at:

- **The development of the whole child and the need to look at individualized instruction and portfolio assessment for every student. We recognize the need for schools to prepare a diverse student population for the 21st century.**

- **The changing global economy and society. What students need to know and be able to do is being altered because of transformations in the United States and the global society.**

- **The need to rethink the learning day and the importance of bridging school and community. Principals need to create partnerships with community agencies and organizations to enhance instructional programs and learning experiences for students in and out of school and to contribute to youth development.**

- **The increasing amounts of data available and the need to translate abundant information into useful knowledge. The education world has been generating volumes of data; the challenge is to turn that data into information that is useful in improving classrooms and schools.**

Finally, NAESP is committed to expanding our own leadership role. We call for new and additional sources of support to help school leaders manage the transition to their new roles and to prepare new leaders for the 21st century. We know that if principals are expected to continuously improve their performance and that of adults and students in learning communities, transformations will be needed in school systems and communities, and new sources of support will be required at all levels.

We stand ready to advocate for these changes. We are committed as a national association to provide research, professional development, supports and learning networks that will help principals and learning communities achieve their desired results for every child.

# How To Use This Guide

**T**his second edition of *Leading Learning Communities* is written and designed as a guide to provide content, tools and resources that principals can use to help meet their individual goals and to lead learning communities so that students and adults are performing at high levels.

While the guide was not created as an evaluation tool, we hope the publication will be a reflection tool and a resource for principals and learning communities, and that others interested in school improvement will use it too—whether they are school board members, superintendents, professors of education, teachers or parents.

Some important elements of the guide include:

**Aligned content of the standards.** Principals who are striving to meet national and state standards will be working toward the standards in this book as well. We've aligned the standards in *Leading Learning Communities* with standards in the first edition from NAESP, with those of the Educational Leadership Policy Standards (formerly known as the Interstate School Leaders Licensure Consortium Standards), and with the performance standards for principals in leading-edge states, such as Arkansas, Florida and Illinois.

Leadership and management permeate these standards, which cannot be implemented piecemeal, but rather should be integrated. Think of the standards as a recipe for creating good schools, not as a menu from which to pick and choose.

**Examples from real schools.** We've designed this guide to represent the voices of principals who helped develop these ideas. No one speaks with more authority about school leadership than principals themselves. Principals are honest, compelling spokespeople for the challenges and opportunities in their profession. In addition, we have found examples of sites that illustrate that the concepts here really work. Each chapter includes stories of real people in real schools that exemplify the ideas outlined in this guide. We expect the readers of this guide to come from all kinds of schools, so we've used examples across a wide geographic and demographic spectrum.

**Reflection and self-assessment.** In the spirit of continuous improvement, we've designed the guide to encourage reflection and self-examination. Each standard section contains a list of practical guiding questions principals can use for individual reflection or to stimulate discussions with staff. In addition, each standard in this second edition includes a tool to help schools identify action steps needed to increase student and adult learning.

We've also included a leadership self-assessment continuum for each standard. The continuum describes—for each strategy of each standard—a journey of development and growth that depicts changes in leadership over time. Principals might use this continuum to assess their own development each year. They also might use it with school faculties to identify current practice compared to desired results and to define professional growth plans, for individuals and the school community. Each continuum is not intended to be prescriptive but rather to support individual principals and school communities as they create a developmental path toward excellence. We recommend focusing on one or two areas each year, identifying areas of strength and setting reasonable and achievable goals for improvement.

**Tools, research and resources.** This guide is evidence-based. We surveyed research literature and spoke with leading thinkers and practitioners who know what works in schools. We've identified specific tools—along with print and online resources— aligned to each standard to help principals and members of learning communities develop strategies to meet the standards. In addition, because readers of the first edition of *Leading Learning Communities* tell us that they continually refer to the research sections for relevant and useful information, we've highlighted targeted and pertinent research that can help principals and faculty members extend their learning and knowledge.

Whether you browse from standard to standard, or work your way straight through, we hope this guide will be helpful to you as a ready resource for school improvement planning and for identifying ongoing professional learning needs.

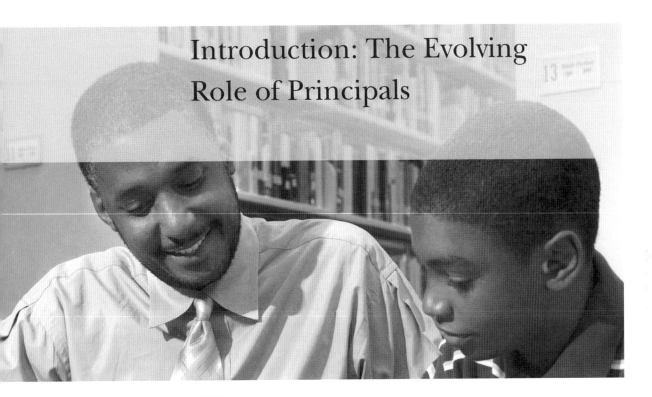

# Introduction: The Evolving Role of Principals

**T**he role of principal continues to become more complex and challenging. Traditional leaders may have considered their jobs to be solely the managers of schools, ensuring that daily operations run smoothly. But the current social and educational context—which combines high-stakes accountability with the high ideals of supporting social, physical and emotional needs of children—demands that all principals demonstrate the vision, courage and skill to lead and advocate for effective learning communities in which all students reach their highest potential.

Still, management remains an important role of principals. In a context of tight local and state budgets, combined with a climate of increased accountability and heightened expectations for student performance, the management of resources—human and financial—in alignment with shared goals for the school is more important than ever before. Every action in the school must support student learning, and all resources must be used wisely and efficiently to support the essential core of instruction.

But we know that the job of principal is more than operational; the work must also be transformational. Principals must require and achieve new levels of performance from themselves, teachers and students. They must understand what students should know and be able to do—and the best instructional practices to teach this content. Beyond knowledge, principals must also have a high capacity to build relationships, forming essential human connections—between principal and teacher, teacher and student, teacher and parent and among all members of the school community.

Effective principals insist on looking at data and analyzing trends, gaps and insights. But they know their role goes beyond actuarial; instead, they must be aspirational. Principals must set and sustain a shared vision for creating a school community that prepares children for a continuously changing society, for college and for the jobs of the future, many of which don't exist yet. Principals also must be motivational, encouraging everyone in the school community to stay focused on continuous improvement and the common values expressed in the school's vision.

Effective principals understand that their jobs are often social and political—requiring new levels of public relations and better marketing of school goals and achievements. The role of principal requires civic participation, including the coordination of services with other community agencies. Principals are respected in the community as a voice for all students and thus are often called on to make the case—locally, statewide and sometimes nationally—for the funding, policies and alignment of values that can ensure equitable access for all students to a high-quality education.

Effective principals never stop teaching, although their focus may have shifted to teaching adults. School leaders create the conditions and structures for learning by providing resources, supports and opportunities for capacity building and continual improvement of performance of adults as well as children. They enable teachers and other staff members to participate in teams, networks and other learning communities—inside and outside the school—sometimes restructuring the school day to make time for these activities. Effective principals know that such learning groups are a necessary opportunity for teachers to read, discuss and share research, collect and analyze data on instructional effectiveness, or conduct action research to test new instructional approaches. Effective principals regularly identify resources to enable teachers to take part in local, regional, and national and international conferences and to visit other classrooms and schools to observe innovative and effective practices.

Overall, principals must be the lead learners in their schools, continuously reading, forecasting predictable scenarios, and analyzing data to assess gaps and possibilities for improvement. They must model learning by reflecting on past experiences and performance as well as focusing on the whole child, and set the tone for every member of the school community that continuous learning is the core business of education.

## Six Standards That Characterize Effective Leaders of Learning Communities

With the help of principals and other education leaders, and through extensive research on emerging knowledge and trends affecting education, NAESP has updated and expanded our standards for what principals should know and be able to do. Individually and collectively, these six standards define leadership for learning communities: places where adults and young people are continuously learning and striving toward improving their knowledge and skills.

Effective leaders of learning communities:

- **Lead schools in a way that places student and adult learning at the center.**

- **Set high expectations for the academic, social, emotional and physical development of all students.**

- **Demand content and instruction that ensure student achievement of agreed-upon standards.**

- **Create a culture of continuous learning for adults tied to student learning and other school goals.**

- **Manage data and knowledge to inform decisions and measure progress of student, adult and school performance.**

- **Actively engage the community to create shared responsibility for student performance and development.**

# Attributes of Effective Learning Communities

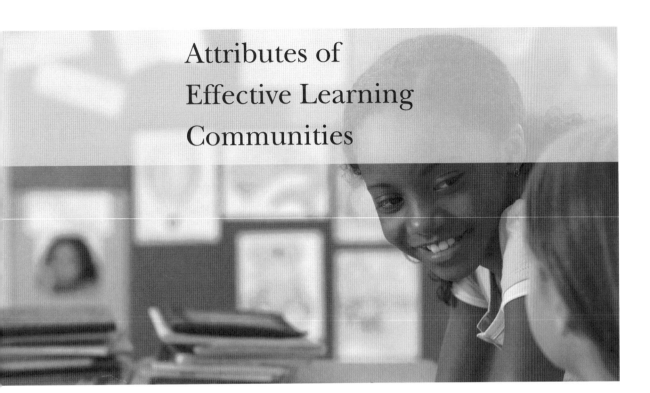

**T**he concept of school as a learning community—or, more appropriately, a collection of numerous nested learning communities—has attracted growing interest since NAESP introduced *Leading Learning Communities* in 2001. We hear from principals, assistant principals, lead teachers and other members of school communities that they are continuing to raise expectations for student learning and for their own performance. As learning communities, they work to identify and apply innovative and effective instructional practices that result in increased student performance. These school leaders embrace the idea of learning from and with each other, and are building and using collaborative structures within schools to do so.

The standards in this document are intended to create a definition of instructional leadership for principals to improve their practice and that of all adults in their learning environment to support high-yield strategies for student learning. In this second edition of *Leading Learning Communities*, standards that have been used successfully by individuals, schools, districts and universities to prepare principals and to support student—and adult— learning in schools have been updated and expanded to align with the ever-changing context in which principals do their work.

NAESP defines learning communities as "places in which adults and students work collaboratively and demonstrate a commitment to continuous improvement of performance." Ultimately, the goal of learning communities is to ensure that all students and adults have the knowledge, skills and capacities to succeed in education, work and life.

NAESP identifies the following core attributes of learning communities:

## Shared Mission, Vision, Values and Goals

The concept of learning communities is founded on a belief that the core mission of public education is not simply to ensure that students are *taught* but to ensure that they *learn*. This shift—from a predominant focus on teaching to a greater emphasis on learning—has profound implications for schools.

An effective learning community adheres to an explicit vision of quality teaching and learning. This vision is consistently articulated and provides a steady guide (our members often refer to their school vision as their "North Star") in making decisions about teaching and learning.

In effective learning communities, students learn through the collaborative, interdependent practice—and continuous learning—of teachers and other adults. Performance outcomes are agreed upon for all students and teachers. Learning community members share transparent values and goals for what students must know and be able to do.

## Commitment to Results

Effective learning communities judge their effectiveness on the basis of results. The daily business of everyone in the school is to work together to improve student and adult performance.

A focus on results requires all members of the learning community to reassess traditional beliefs, assumptions and practices and to test innovative approaches to improving performance. Principals and teachers recognize that data is a powerful indicator of progress. In addition to the traditional approaches of analyzing the progress of student groups, there is an increasing emphasis on using individual data to measure and enhance the success of each learner. By examining the data, members of an effective learning community refuse to ignore or excuse poor performance and honestly confront situations to determine interventions and learning experiences that will improve learner outcomes.

Educators who are committed to results maintain a laser-like focus on student learning. Effectiveness of teaching is assessed against student performance, which often can mean that educators stop assessing themselves by how busy they are or how many programs they participate in. Ongoing common formative assessments are used and scored in consistent ways to facilitate improvement. Results of these assessments are shared among team members.

The question, "Have students made progress toward their learning goals?" resounds throughout an effective learning community.

## Continuous Improvement

Learning community members are engaged in an ongoing cycle of continuous improvement, committed to and persistently reaching toward the organization's ideal vision. Such a commitment is placed within a context in which collective synergy, imagination, spirit, inspiration and continuous learning spur improvement of teaching and learning skills. People in learning communities are driven to constantly expand their competence to produce desired outcomes.

In a learning community of teachers, for instance, each person participates in an ongoing process of identifying the current level of student achievement, establishing a goal to raise that level and working together to achieve it. Teachers evaluate periodic evidence of progress and make sense of the data to determine changes in practice.

## Culture of Collaboration

Isolation is the antithesis of a learning community. Educators in an effective learning community recognize that they must work together to achieve their shared vision of learning for all. They create collaborative structures to support them as they share ideas, materials, lesson plans and strategies. They talk about what's working—and what isn't.

Collaboration goes beyond camaraderie and even beyond cooperation. Many schools have congenial staff members who talk pleasantly with each other and share operational tasks within a school. Members of an effective learning community go farther, joining forces to create and implement a systematic process in which the principal and teachers work together to analyze and improve practice. In effective learning communities, a meaningful and powerful dialogue transforms the school into a place of deep, collective learning and action, which lead to higher levels of performance.

## Collective Inquiry

People who inquire together create community and new knowledge. Reflective dialogue about and collective inquiry into effective practices are key attributes of learning communities. This process includes discussion about curriculum alignment to learning needs, common formative assessments, instructional strategies and ongoing alignment of professional development to school goals. Members of an effective learning community work together to question, search, analyze, develop, test and evaluate new skills, strategies, awareness, attitudes and beliefs that promote student learning. Members challenge and question each other's practice in spirited but optimistic ways. They apply new ideas and information to address learner needs.

## Supportive and Shared Leadership

Some form of facilitative, distributed or shared leadership is essential to an effective support structure for student and adult learning. Transforming a school into a learning community requires the sharing of leadership, power and decision-making while remaining committed to core values and results. Everyone contributes. Everyone learns. Everyone leads.

An effective and sustainable schoolwide learning community requires the complete involvement in learning by principals, all administrators and the teaching, counseling and support staff. School leaders are learners, creating and participating in professional learning opportunities and remaining ever-focused on building their own capacities. Effective leaders model inquiry, investigation, exploration and creative and innovative problem solving for school improvement.

Learning communities are environments in which new relationships are forged between administrators and teachers that lead to collaborative leadership in the school, where all members of the learning community grow professionally and learn to view themselves as leaders and learners.

# Standards and Strategies for Leading Learning Communities

**Standard 1**  Lead schools in a way that places student and adult learning at the center.

Strategies

- **Stay informed of the continually changing context for teaching and learning**
- **Embody learner-centered leadership**
- **Capitalize on the leadership skills of others**
- **Align operations to support student, adult and school learning needs**
- **Advocate for efforts to ensure that policies are aligned to effective teaching and learning**

**Standard 2**  Set high expectations and standards for the academic, social, emotional and physical development of all students.

Strategies

- **Build consensus on a vision that reflects the core values of the school community**
- **Value and use diversity to enhance the learning of the entire school community**
- **Broaden the framework for child development beyond academics**
- **Develop a learning culture that is adaptive, collaborative, innovative and supportive**

**Standard 3**  Demand content and instruction that ensure student achievement of agreed-upon standards.

Strategies

- **Ensure alignment of curriculum with district and school goals, standards, assessments and resources**
- **Invest in a technology-rich culture that connects learning to the global society**
- **Hire, retain and support high-quality teachers**
- **Ensure rigorous, relevant and appropriate instruction for all students**

## Standard 4 — Create a culture of continuous learning for adults tied to student learning and other school goals.

Strategies

- Invest in comprehensive professional development for all adults to support student learning
- Align the schoolwide professional development plan with school and learning goals
- Encourage adults to broaden networks to bring new knowledge and resources to learning environments
- Provide time, structures and opportunities for adults to plan, work, reflect and celebrate together to improve practice

## Standard 5 — Manage data and knowledge to inform decisions and measure progress of student, adult and school performance.

Strategies

- Make performance data a primary driver for school improvement
- Measure student, adult and school performance using a variety of data
- Build capacity of adults and students to use knowledge effectively to make decisions
- Benchmark high-achieving schools with comparable demographics
- Make results transparent to the entire school community

## Standard 6 — Actively engage the community to create shared responsibility for student performance and development.

Strategies

- Engage parents, families and the community to build relationships that support improved performance
- Serve as civic leaders who regularly engage with numerous stakeholders to support students, families and schools in more effective ways
- Shape partnerships to ensure multiple learning opportunities for students, in and out of school
- Market the school's distinctive learning environment and results to inform parents' choices of options that best fit their children's needs
- Advocate for high-quality education for every student

# Lead schools in a way that places student and adult learning at the center.

1 Learning Centered

2 Diverse Communities

3 21st Century Learners

4 Quality Instruction

5 Knowledge and Data

6 Community Engagement

**E**very day, in thousands of schools, effective principals are thinking about how they can best lead and manage multiple systems that together can bring effective practices to scale so that all students—and all adults—achieve better results.

At the core of this work is a relentless focus on learning. Every member of the school community must be continuously learning, including students, educators, families, community partners and citizens. The primary role of the principal is to keep all of these people on a shared journey that makes teaching and learning the core purpose of everyone's work. Whether focused on instruction or operations, effective leaders align every decision to support that shared purpose.

Learner-centered leaders work with a common vision for the high achievement of all children and are clear about their performance results. They insist that every student have access to high-quality, rigorous and relevant 21st century learning. They align all district and community resources—people, time and money—to implement strategic action plans so everyone in the learning community lives that vision. They measure, analyze and discuss data and use it to

No institution can survive it if needs geniuses or supermen to manage it. It must be organized to get along under a leadership of average human beings.

Peter Drucker

make changes needed for progress toward outcomes. This means that the learning community collectively does not allow the press of management or crises to override its attention to learning results.

Being learner-centered means that leaders create processes and structures that enable adults, as well as students, to participate and learn. These leaders are themselves models of continuous learning. They embrace differences as an important contribution—not a hindrance—to learning. And they are committed to increasing their own knowledge, skills and capacities through professional development, peer mentoring, and the establishment and support of schoolwide learning communities.

Principals as members of learning communities share responsibility for achieving expected results. They build on the assets of others in the learning community, both in and out of school. They bring systems thinking and strategic analysis to their efforts. They persistently move effective efforts more broadly and more deeply throughout the school and work to build ownership and sustainability of practices that work. To share learning and knowledge across the learning community, effective leaders create information and administrative systems that align schedules, budgets, facilities, communications, transportation and human resources functions to instruction.

Learner-centered leaders help others understand that they are part of something greater than themselves and provide hope and the belief that, by working together, everyone's performance can improve.

What does it look like when principals lead by putting student and adult learning at the center of schools? We see principals who:

- **Stay informed of the continually changing context for teaching and learning**

- **Embody learner-centered leadership**

- **Capitalize on the leadership skills of others**

- **Align operations to support student, adult and school learning needs**

- **Advocate for efforts to ensure that policies are aligned to effective teaching and learning**

## Stay informed of the continually changing context for teaching and learning

Leaders in all fields need to be current with the emerging trends and knowledge that influence their specific work as well as with the external factors that influence the context of their work. The same is true for principals. Schools do not exist in isolation. Some of the most significant challenges facing learning communities are not coming from schools themselves but from economic, demographic and social trends.

Effective school leaders are continually scanning and mapping various contexts to assess how emerging data and trends will affect their school community. For instance, a change in health care provisions may affect the quality of learning for students. Or, if property taxes are expected to decline, principals might see that school budgets will need to be justified, decreased or re-aligned. Not only do principals need to be aware of these trends, but they also need to make their teachers and parents aware of them.

Knowledgeable principals understand that public education funding is under attack on numerous economic, political and social fronts. They see that market choices for education services for students and families are multiplying in the private and nonprofit sectors. They watch for the implications of local political changes in school board members, superintendents, mayors and members of city and county councils. They foresee the consequences of shifts in local and state budgets.

School leaders need to stay abreast of education trends—whether by reading professional association periodicals and journals, or books, magazines and newspapers; through conversations with peers or experts in particular issues; or through their own action research or professional development experiences. They know that societal shifts in demographics as well as beliefs and values will keep redefining expectations for what constitutes an educated child. As leaders in their profession, effective principals strive to keep up with the speed of new information about brain development, learning styles and effective teaching strategies.

1 Learning Centered
2 Diverse Communities
3 21st Century Learners
4 Quality Instruction
5 Knowledge and Data
6 Community Engagement

## INSIDE A SCHOOL: A FOCUS ON PRACTICE

**Reeds Ferry School, Merrimack, New Hampshire**
**Principal Frank Hoell**

As an educator at Reeds Ferry for 28 years, Frank Hoell knows that to lead a quality elementary school he must share a vision with all individuals involved in the school community. "For me there's a real passion for the principalship and a love of kids and learning," he says. "I work really hard to create that feeling not just from the top down, but from the staff and all the people who deal with the students."

Hoell's vision is focused on just that: love for kids and quality instruction, particularly toward literacy. With the district concerned about literacy, Hoell chose a risky new curriculum that promised literacy improvement. To make the vision work, Hoell knew he had to empower others to lead, which began with identifying a leadership team of four: a reading specialist, counselor, special education advisor and assistant principal. These individuals help Hoell maintain a child-centered building where children know they are respected, heard and challenged. He says he works with the leadership team to "define academic goals, process on things that need to be done and constantly keep the vision in mind: what's working for the students."

Hoell quickly learned this bold vision affected everyone in the school. "We had to ask the teachers to change their teaching style—to change their teaching to the standards," says Hoell, "and we learned that it was our job to help them understand this new focus." Devoting 120 minutes to daily reading and writing has a big impact on schedules, too, and Hoell learned to align resources to help implement the vision. Teachers are given Curriculum Integrated Activity (CIA) time during which they are freed from classroom duties to work with the reading specialist, assistant principal and principal to learn new literacy activities. "For example, we might go over how they develop small group instruction. It helps to have teachers work outside the classroom with their peers," Hoell says.

CIA time also affects other specialists and teachers—counselors, art teachers, gym teachers—who take the students during this time. An art teacher may read a story and then develop an educational art assignment about the main character. "We're showing students that literacy carries over into all disciplines and helping them see the relevance of learning."

## Embody learner-centered leadership

Everything that happens in the school requires both leadership and management and must be directly connected to the learning of students and adults. Principals must manage organizational learning and performance in a way that emphasizes that learning for students and adults is the central function of the school.

Effective leaders know that everyone in the school community is a learner, and that they as principals must not only embrace but also model learning. Starting with their own professional ethics and personal integrity, effective leaders establish a climate of mutual trust and respect that enables all members of a learning community to seek excellence. Effective leaders also know they must help members of their learning communities feel protected: Only when people feel free to take risks can truly creative ideas emerge.

When leaders are learners, they promote equity by acknowledging, respecting and responding to diversity. They communicate the school's learning goals and vision and translate ideas into actions that engage all members of the learning community. They openly discuss the results of data and the need for improvement or changes in practice. They share good news as well as areas that need improvement. They promote an atmosphere of inquiry, reflection and collaboration.

Leaders who are model learners are also deeply committed to their own learning and performance. Such effective leaders embrace a rich understanding of their own work and capacities, and plan and engage in their own professional development as well as that of their staff members.

Major change
is a process of
small wins.

J. Kouzes and
B. Posner

## Capitalize on the leadership skills of others

No matter how experienced a principal is, and regardless of school size, it is simply not possible for one person to have all of the talents necessary to achieve all of a school's goals. Principals who once spent 85 percent to 90 percent of their time managing school operations are now trying hard to spend more time on instructional leadership. Thus, shared authority, accountability and decision-making are essential in a learning community.

Effective leaders know that they must draw on the varied knowledge and capacities of people within the entire school community. To capitalize on this expanded capacity, leaders of learning communities create systems that enable a wide range of people to come up with ideas and carry them out to fulfill the school's vision.

1 Learning Centered

2 Diverse Communities

3 21st Century Learners

4 Quality Instruction

5 Knowledge and Data

6 Community Engagement

In addition, effective leaders know that they need to empower people in order to realize the school's vision. Distributing the leadership functions of innovation, creativity, implementation and accountability for results across the school is more than a nod to current practice; effective leaders know that leadership must be shared if the many administrative and instructional elements of the learning community are to be effective and aligned. Principals whose learning communities have decided to keep their gyms open five nights a week for activities or those who regularly visit classrooms to support instructional improvement know they must make trade-offs in their time and tasks, and that sharing leadership and management is required to do everything well.

Authentic distributed leadership goes beyond sharing responsibilities with the school staff. Parents and other members of the school community often have expertise or time to contribute to learning. Students can be empowered in many ways to support the learning community, whether by leading character education opportunities, celebrations or performances; designing and organizing schoolwide events and activities; conducting focus groups to identify student opinions on important issues; or supporting peer tutoring. Meaningful engagement of students can have a powerful impact on their participation in school and the improvement of the learning community.

By building on the assets of staff, parents, community members and students, effective leaders find that they have the collective expertise and capacity to empower the whole learning community.

## A CLOSER LOOK

### Eight Forces for Leaders of Change

Understanding the process of change is critical for any school leader. According to educational-change expert Michael Fullan, these eight "forces" are key to creating effective and lasting change in school settings:

- **Engaging people's moral purposes**
- **Building capacity**
- **Understanding the change process**
- **Developing cultures for learning**
- **Developing cultures of evaluation**
- **Focusing on leadership for change**
- **Fostering coherence making**
- **Cultivating trilevel development**

Source: Fullan, M., C. Cuttress and A. Kilcher. "8 Forces for Leaders of Change: Presence of the core concepts does not guarantee success, but their absence ensures failure." *Journal of Staff Development.* Vol. 26, No. 4. Oxford, OH: National Staff Development Council, 2005.

## INSIDE A SCHOOL: A FOCUS ON PRACTICE

**Los Peñasquitos Elementary School, San Diego, California**
**Co-Principals Damen Lopez and Jeff King**

At Los Peñasquitos, data is used to guide the school to its goal of "every student, without exception and without excuse, will be proficient or advanced in reading, language arts and math." Co-principals Damen Lopez and Jeff King call this the No Excuses University (NEU), which promotes college readiness for every student through two main focuses: creating a culture of universal achievement and developing exceptional systems.

"We're talking about data in ways we never did," says Lopez. "Every staff member participates in creating plans for assessments and every student is involved in this process." Teachers and administrators collect and analyze classroom data and incorporate results into teacher action plans. Each student in the school has goals that are based on his or her specific measures of data. "Kids are becoming closely involved in knowing and tracking their own data. And teachers are making sure any data they use in their classroom is absolutely driving instruction," Lopez adds.

The entire staff is committed to finding new ways to determine parallels between scores on assessments and the types of intervention needed. By using the data to develop structures for improving instruction, school staff can respond quickly to all students' needs.

The results speak wonders for the NEU at Los Peñasquitos. With 35 different languages spoken at the Title I school, the effective use of data is paying off. "Every subgroup is thriving," Lopez says. "When you talk about how it's affecting success, it's affecting not only our success in the district, but also our success in the state and the country." Los Peñasquitos is one of only 16 schools in San Diego County to obtain the honor of being named a "10-10 school," which means that it earned a "10" ranking among schools statewide and among similar schools.

Lopez and King have developed 14 NEUs across the country. "We're trying to create a revolution," Lopez adds. "We're trying to show educators that there is a system for creating systems. We're showing them strategies today that they can put into practice tomorrow."

1 Learning Centered

2 Diverse Communities

3 21st Century Learners

4 Quality Instruction

5 Knowledge and Data

6 Community Engagement

## Align operations to support student, adult and school learning needs

To create a learning community, effective principals know that their school—as an organization with many responsibilities and employees—needs to be managed well. Carrying out a vision for a well-managed learning community requires careful planning to ensure that the school's resources match its priorities. Doing so not only helps ensure that the school makes progress toward its vision, but also signals to the community that the principal and the school leadership consider the vision to be the school's "True North" and are committed to honoring shared values.

## A CLOSER LOOK

### Responsibilities That Impact Student Achievement

After examining studies on school leadership, researchers at Mid-continent Research for Education and Learning (McREL) concluded there is a significant link between school-level leadership and student achievement. What's more, while school leaders can have a positive impact on achievement, they can also have a *negative* impact on achievement by concentrating on the wrong practices, or by misinterpreting the magnitude of a change in practice.

The McREL school leadership study found 21 leadership responsibilities and 66 practices that positively affected student achievement. The 21 responsibilities are the basis for a framework that describes the knowledge, skills, strategies and tools leaders need to positively affect student achievement, including:

- Culture
- Order
- Discipline
- Resources
- Involvement in curriculum, instruction and assessment
- Focus

- Knowledge of curriculum, instruction and assessment
- Visibility
- Contingent rewards
- Communication
- Outreach
- Input
- Affirmation

- Relationship
- Change agent
- Optimizer
- Ideals/beliefs
- Monitors/evaluates
- Flexibility
- Situational awareness
- Intellectual stimulation

Source: Waters, T., R. Marzano and B. McNulty. *Balanced Leadership: What 30 Years of Research Tells Us About the Effect of Leadership on Student Achievement.* Denver, CO: McREL, 2003.

Effective principals know that to run a high-performing school, every resource—time, people and money—must be managed in ways that explicitly support and increase learning for students and adults. Cost-efficiency and effectiveness must be measured in terms of impact on achieving the school's learning goals. This requires regular examination of all operational systems and the alignment of those systems to the instructional program.

Effective leaders have long been skillful at securing foundation grants, community resources or district funds to supplement their budgets. But each resource comes with its own management requirements. Filling resource gaps requires more than identifying new dollars and partners; it requires making sure that new projects and initiatives will advance the school's learning objectives.

The management of operational functions—facilities, transportation, budgets, safety, utilities, food services and schedules—must meet standards of performance within their industries. Some large urban schools have identified a second person, either an employee or community volunteer, to run the operations of a school. These school administration managers, or SAMs, are generally deployed to manage the duties of a school so principals can devote at least 70 percent of their time to instructional matters. In Louisville, Kentucky, for example, SAMs help principals keep focused on instructional tasks—clear learning goals, congruency, diagnoses of prior learning, task analysis, direct response and mid-course corrections.

Management of personnel remains the responsibility of the school leader, who must determine the best assignment of teachers, staff and stakeholders to achieve student learning goals. Effective leaders of high-performing schools are skilled in the flexible use of the talents of all adults to ensure the most efficient operation of the school in achieving its performance targets for student and adult learning.

The distributed view of leadership shifts focus from school principals and other formal and informal leaders to the web of leaders, followers and the situation that gives form to leadership practice.

J. Spillane and J. Diamond

Learning Centered **1**

Diverse Communities **2**

21st Century Learners **3**

Quality Instruction **4**

Knowledge and Data **5**

Community Engagement **6**

A CLOSER LOOK

## Distinguished Educator Programs

Two states—Kentucky and Pennsylvania—are helping struggling school districts tackle poor student achievement by providing assistance from specially trained teams of educators. To fend off more drastic interventions under the No Child Left Behind (NCLB) Act, the distinguished educator teams target the district level to ensure a systemic approach to change.

In Kentucky, there is a long history of working individually with low-performing schools, but only recently has there been a shift to the district level. Kentucky's distinguished educator team includes a staff member from the state department of education, a "highly skilled educator" selected by the state department of education, a school board member from another district selected by the Kentucky School Boards Association and a retired superintendent selected by the Kentucky Association of School Administrators. Each of the members has a successful track record in raising student achievement.

Pennsylvania's program, launched in 2006, provides struggling districts with a team of six former principals and district administrators who generally split their time between two low-achieving districts.

In just a short time, distinguished educator teams in both states have worked with poor-performing districts to implement systemic changes: conducting audits to determine strengths and weaknesses; reallocating staff; working with the districts to develop policy; and crafting new data-management systems. While it is too early to determine the impact on student achievement, district and school leaders who are taking part in the programs report positive changes in the overall culture and management of the districts, and a more comprehensive and cohesive plan of action for addressing shortcomings.

Source: Edwards, V. B. *Leading for Learning.* Supplement to the September 23, 2006, issue of *Education Week.* Bethesda, MD: Editorial Projects in Education, 2006.

1 Learning Centered
2 Diverse Communities
3 21st Century Learners
4 Quality Instruction
5 Knowledge and Data
6 Community Engagement

## Advocate for efforts to ensure that policies are aligned to effective teaching and learning

Sometimes achieving a school's vision requires more than a change in school practices and behaviors. For instance, a school community might want to achieve goals that the school system's curriculum or assessment program does not support. While school leaders can make some changes to align curriculum and instruction to their school's vision, they often can do little, by themselves, to change district policy.

Effective school leaders use their voice and position to inform other school and community leaders about the need for change, and often build coalitions with other leaders to develop new policies that serve students in their school and across the district. These principals know that if the vision truly reflects the school community's values, the community is likely to endorse efforts to strengthen such policies.

While advocating for policy change at state and federal levels is not their direct responsibility, effective leaders recognize that they are a trusted voice among their peers, teachers and community members on learning issues. They use their voice wisely, to move beyond compliance and illuminate policies needed to achieve the best possible learning for students and adults. For instance, effective leaders participate in peer networks to bring to the table the voices of principals, teachers and students to define and advocate for relevant professional development practices.

## Standard 1: Reflection Questions

1. How can we stay ahead of upcoming changes within other sectors of the ⌐ community that have implications for teaching practices and learning resource supports for students and families?

2. How can we more effectively use the leadership skills of every staff member to *Collab* improve teaching and learning for students and adults?

3. Do students, teachers, staff and community partners describe the leadership culture of the school as encouraging and supportive of leadership by others beyond the principal?

4. How can the school's operations be more effectively managed so the principal *Analy* can spend more time being an instructional leader?

5. What processes exist or need to exist to ensure that allocation of resources is directly tied to supporting high-performance teaching and learning?

6. Does each stakeholder group that interacts with students and teachers describe the results of its interactions in terms of new learning?

7. Who currently needs to hear the school leader's voice to ensure that district and community policies support effective teaching and learning?

# Standard 1: Action Steps

After answering the Reflection Questions, list the Action Steps needed to attain the learning goals specific to each question:

| Reflection Question | Action Step(s) | Who needs to take the lead? Who needs to be involved? |
|---|---|---|
| 1 | | |
| 2 | | |
| 3 | | |
| 4 | | |
| 5 | | |
| 6 | | |
| 7 | | |

1 Learning Centered
2 Diverse Communities
3 21st Century Learners
4 Quality Instruction
5 Knowledge and Data
6 Community Engagement

# Standard 1: Leadership Continuum

This self-assessment continuum is intended to help you move toward higher levels of leadership. Consider using this tool at the beginning of the school year and again at the end to assess areas of growth and to identify needed areas of personal and behavioral change.

| Strategy | Level 1 | Level 2 | Level 3 | Level 4 | Level 5 | Score Circle One |
|---|---|---|---|---|---|---|
| **1. Stay informed of the continually changing context for teaching and learning.** | The principal does not formally scan or map district or societal changes. | The principal provides a description of the district or community context for teaching and learning in response to a local, state, national or federal requirement. | The principal alerts teachers about societal changes that may have an immediate impact on teaching and learning and initiates dialogue to determine action needed. | The principal and teacher leaders regularly scan changes in the political, social and economic sectors of the district and local, state and national communities to determine the changes most likely to affect teaching and learning efforts. | The principal has established a schoolwide culture of regular discourse about emerging knowledge, trends and changes in the society, and identification of short- and long-term implications for attaining the school's vision. | 1 2 3 4 5 |
| **2. Embody learner-centered leadership.** | The principal and teachers assume some students will learn and some will not. | The principal provides a description of leadership and learning in response to a local, state, national or federal requirement. | The principal and most teachers evidence leadership that focuses on learning results for both students and adults, and shapes a continuous learning culture through the creation of learning communities. | The principal, teachers and students show ownership of their own learning and the learning of others. Learning communities collaborate in examining student and adult learning results and effective practices. | Everyone in the school community is expected to be a continuous learner. The learning culture exhibits core values of: reflection, inquiry, shared understanding, collaboration, emerging knowledge, excellence in results and advocacy for quality learning. | 1 2 3 4 5 |
| **3. Capitalize on the leadership skills of others.** | The principal "runs" the school, making all decisions with limited participation from staff, while usually leaving instructional decisions to individual teachers. | The principal allows leadership by others to satisfy local, state, national or federal program requirements. | The principal identifies key teacher leaders to guide learning communities, distributing leadership and developing a culture that supports creative risk-taking and requires input from all stakeholders. | The principal and key leaders model collaborative leadership by engaging the leadership skills of others to develop and advance learning community efforts to improve practices to attain the school vision. | A shared leadership culture builds on the alignment of everyone's leadership style, skill and experience, based on the work to be done. Shared leadership creates shared responsibility for implementation and accountability for learning results. | 1 2 3 4 5 |

1 Learning Centered
2 Diverse Communities
3 21st Century Learners
4 Quality Instruction
5 Knowledge and Data
6 Community Engagement

| Strategy | Level 1 | Level 2 | Level 3 | Level 4 | Level 5 | Score Circle One |
|---|---|---|---|---|---|---|
| 4. Align operations to support student, adult and school learning needs. | The principal makes decisions about the schedules, teacher assignments and financial resource allocations with little or no input from others and no explicit connection to student learning needs. | The principal alters schedules, teacher assignments and financial allocations based on criteria and requirements provided by local, state, national and federal programs with limited input from teachers, staff, students or community members. | The principal and teacher leaders make joint decisions to change schedules, teacher assignments and allocation of resources based on student learning needs of some student groups and teacher needs to plan and learn together in learning communities. | The principal and teacher leaders engage other faculty and some community members to adapt teacher assignments, in-school and out-of-school schedules and allocation of school and community resources based on group and individual student learning needs. | The principal, teachers, staff, students and stakeholders ensure in-school and out-of-school allocation of resources—time, people, financial—is equitable and determined by student learning needs—academic, emotional, social and physical. Schedules, assignments and resources are aligned to the changing learning needs of students, adults and the school community. | 1 2 3 4 5 |
| 5. Advocate for efforts to ensure that policies are aligned to effective teaching and learning. | There is very limited intentional connection between community policies and effective teaching and learning. | The principal may need to advocate for policies to support effective teaching and learning to meet local, state, national or federal legal or partnership requirements. | The principal engages community leaders about community policies that support or block effective teaching and learning and attainment of the school's vision. | The principal and some teachers or stakeholders help shape community policies to better support attainment of the school's vision for both in-school and out-of-school learning experiences. | School, district and community leaders engage in ongoing dialogue, advocacy and action for changes in local, state, national and federal policies that support high performance of students and adults. | 1 2 3 4 5 |

# For More Information

## On the Web

**Jim Collins** (www.jimcollins.com), a leading researcher on what it takes to build great companies, presents a series of principles in his book, *Good to Great: Why Some Companies Make the Leap . . . And Others Don't*, that have caught the attention of schools. His Web site contains exercises, audio files and other resources that can help schools achieve greatness in education.

**KnowledgeWorks Foundation and the Institute for the Future** present an online interactive map (www. kwfdn.org/map) about the future forces affecting education. This provocative tool helps visitors to visualize trends and issues that will shape learning.

## Resources and Research

**Fullan, M.** *Leading in a Culture of Change.* **San Francisco: Jossey-Bass, 2007.**

The author provides leaders with insights into the dynamics of change. He integrates five core competencies: attending to a broader moral purpose; keeping on top of the change process; cultivating relationships; sharing knowledge; and setting a vision and context for creating coherence.

**Goldring, E., A. Porter, J. Murphy, S. Elliott and X. Cravens.** *Assessing Learning-Centered Leadership: Connections to Research, Professional Standards, and Current Practices.* **Nashville, TN: Vanderbilt University, 2007.**

The report focuses on topics related to instructional leadership and explores leader behaviors that can improve learning. It discusses *what* principals or leadership teams must accomplish to improve academic and social learning for all students, and *how* they create those core components.

**Spillane, J., and J. Diamond, eds.** *Distributed Leadership in Practice.* **New York: Teachers College Press, 2007.**

Based on extensive research and a rich theoretical perspective developed by experts in the field, this book examines what it means to take a distributed approach to leadership. Including numerous case studies of individual schools, it explores how taking a distributed perspective can help researchers understand and connect more directly to leadership practice and illustrates that the day-to-day practice of leadership is an important line of inquiry for those interested in improving school leadership.

**Wagner, T., R. Kegan, L. Laskow Lahey, R. Lemons, J. Garnier, D. Helsing, A. Howell and H. Thurber Rasmussen.** *Change Leadership: A Practical Guide to Transforming Our Schools.* **San Francisco: Jossey-Bass, 2005.**

The authors help leaders successfully navigate the change process. Two core capacities are discussed: leaders need to learn how to take effective action—while facing resistance—to help schools become what they need to be and leaders need to learn how to help individuals change to better serve school communities.

**Waters, T., and G. Cameron.** *The Balanced Leadership Framework: Connecting Vision with Action.* **Denver, CO: McREL, 2006.**

This handbook helps apply the lessons learned in *Balanced Leadership: What 30 Years of Leadership Tells Us About the Effect of Leadership on Student Achievement* (McREL, 2003), which highlights 21 responsibilities of effective leadership. The book organizes the 21 responsibilities into three components: focus of leadership, building a purposeful community and magnitude of change.

Standard **2**

# Set high expectations and standards for the academic, social, emotional and physical development of all students.

1 Learning Centered

2 Diverse Communities

3 21st Century Learners

4 Quality Instruction

5 Knowledge and Data

6 Community Engagement

**T**he phrase "all children can learn at high levels" may have become commonplace, but achieving it is rare. An increase in the diversity of students—including English language learners, students with disabilities and students from low-income homes—poses particular challenges for schools, because these students are among those who have been least well served in the past.

The No Child Left Behind (NCLB) Act raised expectations for many schools by requiring all students to reach proficiency in reading and mathematics by 2014. But students need a broad set of knowledge and skills in addition to reading and math. And all schools must continuously expect higher levels of learning for all students, even those who have already attained proficiency.

To deliver on the promise of high levels of learning for all students, particularly with an increasingly diverse student population, principals will have to lead schools that individualize learning, according to Michael Fullan, professor emeritus of education at the

Five years of effective teaching can completely close the gap between low-income students and others.

R. Marzano, J. Kain and E. Hunushek

University of Ontario. "You have to look at who your students are," he says. "When we talk about assessment for learning, it's the ability to differentiate the learning [that matters]. The different cultural backgrounds have special needs. This means that schools have to relate to every child and where they come from."

As a result, principals must make greater efforts than in the past to understand their students and the communities from which they come—while maintaining their commitment to ensuring that all students learn at high levels. They must examine their beliefs about ethnic and socio-economic groups and persuade teachers to do the same. Such efforts serve to overcome stereotypes and help school leaders understand how diverse backgrounds can enhance a school's learning environment and create a positive learning culture for the entire school community. Professional development experiences need to make the explicit connection between learning expectations, effective teaching and high student performance.

In addition, effective leaders know that, beyond academics, the social, emotional and physical development of children is essential. Principals encourage the development of the whole child by supporting the physical and mental health of children, as well as their social and emotional well-being and their sense of safety and self-confidence. Leaders often do this by providing a connection between the school and the broader community.

What does it look like when principals lead diverse communities? We see principals who:

- **Build consensus on a vision that reflects the core values of the school community**

- **Value and use diversity to enhance the learning of the entire school community**

- **Broaden the framework for child development beyond academics**

- **Develop a learning culture that is adaptive, collaborative, innovative and supportive**

## INSIDE A SCHOOL: A FOCUS ON PRACTICE

### Thomson Elementary School, Washington, D.C.
### Principal Gladys Camp

Gladys Camp, principal at Thomson Elementary, focuses on knowing the community that her school serves. Located next to Chinatown, and serving a diverse student and teacher population, the school has instituted the first Chinese language program in its district.

"We have an ESL population of 202 out of 386 students. We chose Chinese to increase the number of languages that our children are learning—now some are learning three different languages," says Camp.

To Camp, it's important that the students not just learn the language, but also understand the different cultures and ethnicities that surround them. "We have a ValuesFirst Program that focuses on respect, responsibility and tolerance. Through the use of a diversity calendar, we hold monthly celebrations that focus on different ethnic groups—from Hispanic Heritage Month to Black History Month to Native American Month. We truly honor our diversity."

Acknowledging the challenges of representing a diverse community, Camp also strives to find opportunities that expand her ability to lead her teachers to cultural competence. Thomson was selected along with four other schools to be part of an agreement with the Chinese government, affording Camp a trip to China over the 2007 summer. One teacher was given a Fulbright award to study in the country for five weeks.

It doesn't stop there. Taking advantage of the vast cultural offerings of Washington, D.C. , Camp also partners with several embassy programs. So far, she and her staff have worked with Norway, Turkey and China.

"My staff is diverse," Camp adds. "We receive professional development on multiculturalism, and learn how to help each other and our students embrace all cultures. Many staff, myself included, have enrolled in Spanish classes to better relate to our Spanish-speaking parents and students."

1 Learning Centered
2 Diverse Communities
3 21st Century Learners
4 Quality Instruction
5 Knowledge and Data
6 Community Engagement

## Build consensus on a vision that reflects the core values of the school community

The first step to ensuring that all students learn at high levels is to set a collective expectation that they will do so—regardless of their backgrounds. Effective principals know that the higher the standards their school targets, the better the chances of sustaining a long-term commitment to continuous improvement of teaching and learning.

While leadership sets a parameter of high expectations for the school, the principal cannot impose a vision of how to get there. Effective leaders know that people will strive to attain only something for which they feel ownership, so a principal's task is to create a consensus vision that all members of a school community can support and work collaboratively to reach. To create consensus, effective leaders bring together a wide range of stakeholders within the school community, listen to their aspirations and work with them to craft a vision that reflects shared values.

Once set, a vision of high expectations for all must pervade every aspect of a school, centered around the school's primary tasks: ensuring high levels of student learning and creating safe, motivating learning environments for every student. A long-term vision that includes college-readiness standards for all students—including disadvantaged students—can also promote equity and the closing of achievement gaps. Advantaged students in affluent areas are focused on and in many cases have already exceeded these standards. Schools that expect less of disadvantaged students have, in effect, given up on closing achievement gaps and educating all students.

Leading with vision takes more than simply articulating a set of goals. Effective leaders recognize that implementing a vision is likely to demand new ways of doing business, and they are not afraid to try bold approaches to improve the school's ability to get more students learning at higher levels. Indeed, having a shared vision for high performance for all can give everyone in the learning community license to try innovative strategies.

# A CLOSER LOOK

## Serving Gifted Students

With so much attention focused on students reaching proficiency, gifted students are often overlooked. The National Association for Gifted Children (NAGC) has developed resources for school leaders on the identification of gifted students, program development, curriculum and instruction, guidance, professional development and evaluation for gifted children. Here are some reflection questions presented by NAGC for school leaders to consider:

- **What are the dangers in failing to provide gifted learners with rigorous, challenging curriculum?**

- **When was the last time that your school or district policies related to gifted education were reviewed and revised?**

- **Describe five different ways in which a student might demonstrate proficiency, thereby indicating a need for acceleration and/or differentiation.**

- **Review your school's acceleration policy. Does it provide written policies related to the following: grade skipping; subject acceleration; early entrance to kindergarten, middle school, high school and college; dual enrollment; and Advanced Placement (AP) courses?**

- **What criteria would you use to select resources and materials for a gifted program?**

- **How do gifted students benefit from having access to a counselor who is familiar with the characteristics and socio-emotional needs of gifted learners?**

- **How might you respond to a gifted student who is underachieving in your classroom?**

- **Brainstorm a list of available resources to help you better communicate with parents and community members who are not fluent in English.**

- **What potential concerns should be raised with a district that uses a 15-year-old test to identify students for its gifted program?**

- **Who are the stakeholders related to your gifted program? What evaluation questions would each group want to investigate?**

For more standards and tools for gifted education see: www.nagc.org.

Source: National Association for Gifted Children (www.nagc.org).

1 Learning Centered
2 Diverse Communities
3 21st Century Learners
4 Quality Instruction
5 Knowledge and Data
6 Community Engagement

In addition to integrating the vision into all aspects of teaching and learning, effective leaders regularly revisit the vision. Circumstances perpetually change: The school's student population might shift, or the community might undergo an economic transition. When changes occur, the school vision must shift to reflect the new reality.

Expecting all students to learn at high levels requires the entire school staff to take responsibility for fulfilling those expectations. Harvard Graduate School of Education's Richard Elmore uses the phrase "internal accountability" to describe school staff members' shared belief that they are accountable for the success of every student. Accountable professionals take responsibility for making sure they do everything they can to improve learning, and frequently monitor and evaluate student and school performance to make sure they are meeting their goals.

## A CLOSER LOOK

### Working Toward a More Inclusive Society

The National Federation for Just Communities (www.federationforjustcommunities.org) works with member organizations in more than 15 states to bring the values of diversity, inclusion and social justice to communities, schools, workplaces and institutions. Efforts focus on a range of educational programs, trainings and conferences targeted to different audiences. For example:

- **In California, school leaders can take part in the Institute for Equity in Education offered through Just Communities, Central Coast. The institute is a three-and-a-half-day program in which school leaders explore issues related to race and difference, and identify strategies for addressing institutional racism, educational inequality and achievement gaps in schools.**

- **In Ohio, students can take part in ACT—Action and Awareness for Change Teams. The program empowers students with the skills and resources to serve as change agents for inclusion. The Diversity Center of Northeast Ohio works with 10 middle schools and 10 high schools each year, focusing on curriculum and lessons that are linked to the state's academic standards.**

- **The Michigan Roundtable for Diversity & Inclusion offers opportunities for teachers in Detroit to take part in the LINC Leadership Institute. Developed to improve student achievement, the program uses service learning as a tool for integrating diversity education into the classroom and establishing a respectful, inclusive culture within the school. Schools receive technical assistance throughout the school year, providing teachers with resources to develop activities, implement the practices in the classroom, and evaluate and assess the outcomes.**

Sources: National Federation for Just Communities; Just Communities, Central Coast; The Diversity Center of Northeast Ohio; and The Michigan Roundtable for Diversity & Inclusion.

When the pressure is on to improve, schools with internal accountability can do so. Schools with high levels of internal accountability are better able than those with low levels of internal accountability—those that tend to point to students' backgrounds as the source of their difficulties—to respond effectively to external accountability systems. Schools with strong internal accountability also set high expectations for adult learning.

## Value and use diversity to enhance the learning of the entire school community

Valuing diversity means accepting and respecting differences. People come from very different backgrounds, and their customs, thoughts, communication styles, values, traditions and institutions vary accordingly. Cultural experiences influence choices that range from recreational activities to subjects of study. Even how one chooses to define family is determined by culture.

Diversity among cultures must be recognized, as should the diversity within them. Individuals are exposed to many different cultures through school, work, television, technology, books and other avenues. People generally assume a common culture is shared among members of racial, linguistic and religious groups. Indeed, the larger group may share common historical and geographical experiences, but individuals may share nothing beyond similar physical appearance, language or spiritual beliefs. In addition to defining diversity by class, gender, ethnicity or race, effective leaders also look for diversity in how people learn, and how age, beliefs, perspectives and experiences influence learning.

 **TERMS TO KNOW**

### A Whole Child

The Commission on the Whole Child says that a "whole child" is …

- **Intellectually active**
- **Physically, verbally, socially and academically competent**
- **Empathetic, kind, caring and fair**
- **Creative and curious**
- **Disciplined, self-directed and goal-oriented**
- **Free**
- **A critical thinker**
- **Confident**
- **Cared for and valued**

Source: Commission on the Whole Child. *The Learning Compact Redefined: A Call to Action.* Alexandria, VA: Association for Supervision and Curriculum Development, 2007.

1 Learning Centered
2 Diverse Communities
3 21st Century Learners
4 Quality Instruction
5 Knowledge and Data
6 Community Engagement

The increasing diversity of the student population has far-reaching implications for how students learn and how adults teach. Diversity affects the education and social dynamics within schools, as the student population looks less and less like the teacher and principal work force. The proportion of minority teachers and principals has historically not kept pace with the increase in the minority student population.

Effective leaders who value diversity persistently build within their school communities an understanding of cultures and an ability to effectively teach students from different backgrounds. The term "cultural competence" was first used in connection with health care, referring to the ability to provide services that are respectful of and responsive to the cultural and linguistic needs of a patient. In the field of education, the term means that educators and everyone in a school community should have access to supports to communicate with non-English-speaking students or parents and should take into account cultural habits when constructing an educational plan for individual students.

## A CLOSER LOOK

### Supporting English Language Learners

Building a responsive learning environment is key to the success of English language learners (ELLs). The Education Alliance at Brown University suggests nine principles that will support a high-quality ELL environment. ELLs are most successful when:

- **School leaders, administrators and educators recognize that educating ELLs is the responsibility of the entire school staff.**
- **Educators recognize that ELLs are a heterogeneous group that differs greatly in linguistic, cultural, social, familial and personal backgrounds.**
- **Students' languages and cultures are utilized as a resource for further learning.**
- **There are strong links connecting home, school and community.**
- **ELLs are afforded equitable access to school resources and programs.**
- **There are high expectations of all ELLs.**
- **There are qualified teachers who are well-prepared and willing to work with ELLs.**
- **Language and literacy are infused throughout the educational process, including in curriculum and instruction.**
- **Assessment is valid and purposeful and includes consideration of both first- and second-language literacy development.**

Source: Vialpando, J., J. Yedlin, C. Linse, M. Harrington and G. Cannon. *Educating English Language Learners: Implementing Instructional Practices.* Providence, RI: The National Council of La Raza and The Education Alliance at Brown University, 2005.

School communities that are culturally competent are those that value diversity. Adults who are respectful of and responsive to cultural needs are those who continually assess their own beliefs, biases and knowledge about cultures. These adults are conscious of the implications and consequences when cultures interact. In addition, competence in dealing with diversity requires an ability to adapt environments or instruction when needed. Cultural competence in schools requires an integration and transformation of knowledge about individuals and groups into specific standards, policies, practices and attitudes. These components can then be used to construct appropriate learning environments, and to improve the quality of relationships and the delivery of instruction—all of which can add up to better outcomes.

## Broaden the framework for child development beyond academics

The factors identified as contributing to environmental richness—socialization, physical activity and mental stimulation—are tied closely to the notion of enriching learning environments. In varying degrees, these factors must all be accommodated within the school day and within school schedules and programs. They reflect, and provide evidence to support, what many education leaders believe about students and learning: Rigorous and relevant curriculum and instruction—supported by strong relationships and a welcoming learning environment—matter.

Life success requires more than academic success; it requires that children feel a sense of emotional and social well-being. The State Department of Education in Illinois has identified five key elements—self-awareness, self-management, social awareness, interpersonal skills and responsible decision-making skills—that children need to be steeped in to help ensure they have the mindset to become successful learners. And a number of other states have begun to include standards that support educating students in character development, physical fitness, and the knowledge and skills of citizenship.

According to Willard Daggett of the International Center for Leadership in Education, effective school leaders know that humans are social creatures and that socialization based on strong relationships—between and among students, among students and staff, and with the larger community outside the school—is critical to optimizing growth for every individual. Socialization is also critical in language development, in the sharing and exchange of ideas, and in fostering creativity.

The question is not, 'Is it possible to educate all children well?' But rather, 'Do we want to do it badly enough?'

Deborah Meier

Effective leaders know that learning takes place not only in school. Nonacademic skills can be built through community and out-of-school learning opportunities increasingly available in after-school programs, cultural institutions, business and industry, and community organizations. Effective leaders blend all types of learning in and out of school, and bring explicit attention to the developmental needs of the whole child by identifying out-of-school learning opportunities that support and extend academic learning.

Many parents also have taken extraordinary efforts to expose their children to a wide range of opportunities for learning beyond the school day. The challenge is that all students need these extended learning opportunities, but many students and families do not know how to access them or lack the financial resources or transportation that enables participation. In an authentic learning community, these extended learning opportunities need to be identified and made accessible to all students.

## A CLOSER LOOK

### A New Day for Learning

The Time, Learning, and Afterschool Task Force, chaired by former NAESP Executive Director Vincent Ferrandino, developed a new concept of learning that focuses on:

- **Redefining student success**
- **Using research-based knowledge about how children learn best**
- **Integrating proven strategies for acquiring and reinforcing knowledge throughout a student's learning day**
- **Building new collaborative structures across communities and up and down governance levels**
- **Creating new opportunities for leadership and professional development**

Schools nationwide are making strides using elements of the all-day, year-round learning concept. Dallas ArtsPartners is a program that provides elementary school students with access to arts, humanities and sciences through community partnerships. Program evaluations have found that for each year of participation in the program, African-American and Latino students outperformed their peers on standardized reading tests. Citizen Schools, based in Boston, provides programming for 2,000 middle school students at 30 sites in five different states. Students gain hands-on training by becoming apprentices, working with adult mentors after school. As with ArtsPartners, Citizen Schools is seeing positive results: students in the program had higher grades and test scores, less absenteeism and better behavior in school than their peers not in the program.

Source: Time, Learning, and Afterschool Task Force. *A New Day for Learning.* Washington, D.C. : Time, Learning, and Afterschool Task Force, 2007.

1 Learning Centered
2 Diverse Communities
3 21st Century Learners
4 Quality Instruction
5 Knowledge and Data
6 Community Engagement

## Develop a learning culture that is adaptive, collaborative, innovative and supportive

Effective leaders create communities of learners—both adult and student—who read, research, develop and test innovative approaches. Leaders develop healthy learning cultures in which networks of adults share ideas and knowledge, and study and analyze student performance data.

An example of an adaptive learning culture is one in which individual learning plans are used for all students. For decades, schools have conducted a variety of assessments for students with disabilities to determine their learning needs, and have crafted, along with parents, an Individualized Education Program (IEP) for each student that reflects the assessment results. IEPs include goals for students and define the instructional approaches that schools will use to help students with disabilities achieve their goals.

Educators increasingly recognize that this approach is valuable for *all* students. Each student has a unique set of knowledge and skills and his or her own learning needs, and teachers must understand every student's learning background, particularly in schools with high rates of mobility, where students arrive at school throughout the year. Each student takes a different path to reach high levels of learning, depending on the knowledge and skills on which each student builds.

## INSIDE A SCHOOL: A FOCUS ON PRACTICE

### Odyssey Elementary, Everett, Washington
### Principal Cheryl Boze

Odyssey Elementary is one of many schools across the country working with an increasingly diverse student and parent population. "Twelve years ago we had 13 students who spoke English as a second language; now we have 250," says Principal Cheryl Boze.

One of the strategies at Odyssey has been a strong focus on outreach, using an approach developed by the Alliance for Better Schools called the Natural Leaders Program. The goal is to reach out to families that have not been very engaged in the school, mainly because of the language barrier, to provide a welcoming environment.

"We identified some parents who were natural leaders in the community and we provided them with special training in how to reach out to their community," says Boze.

The school currently has three Spanish-speaking parents and one Russian/Ukranian-speaking parent serving as leaders. The parents have a list of families they check in with each month, inviting them to special events, keeping them abreast of activities and listening to their concerns.

The parent leaders also host informational meetings for their community—a tactic that has really taken hold in Spanish-speaking neighborhoods. Topics range from understanding the legal system to helping children with homework.

The parent leaders also serve a critical role in helping to translate notes from teachers and school fliers, and working as interpreters during meetings between school staff and parents. As a result, attendance is up, parents are more engaged and they're volunteering in record numbers.

"It used to be that parents who weren't native speakers hardly came to any school events," says Boze, "and now they are so much more comfortable."

Another example of strategies to meet students' diverse learning needs is the use of tiered instructional models. One such approach is known as Response to Intervention (RTI). Under RTI, teachers assess all students and identify those at risk of falling behind. All students are taught the common curriculum using a variety of instructional strategies, and those who are identified as being at risk are monitored. Those who are not making sufficient progress receive different or additional supports, while the teacher continues to monitor their progress. Students who continue to make inadequate instructional progress then receive additional services and supports at the top of the pyramid of interventions that are more intensive and individualized and sometimes focused on behavioral and other nonacademic factors.

Effective leaders support tailored, or differentiated, instruction as a means to enable teachers to address a range of diverse learning needs and characteristics. This requires that members of the school community share the belief that every person has a unique way he or she learns best. Differentiated instruction also requires that teachers have a repertoire of effective practices that can be tailored to different interests, learning styles, experiences, strengths and needs.

As classrooms increase in diversity, the urgency for innovative teaching skills in differentiation also increases. Combined with the rigor of high standards for each student, differentiated instruction is both an art and a science, changing traditional roles of both students and teachers. Differentiated instruction requires a firm commitment to hold students accountable for high levels of learning while creating multiple pathways for students to reach those standards.

In school communities that support differentiated instruction, the learning culture allows teachers to work together to create meaningful learning opportunities. With clarity and grounding in the school's learning objectives, students share responsibility for their own learning, aligned to their own learning goals and styles. Learning cultures in which such instruction exists are often dynamic and energetic—and are sometimes unpredictable. Teachers facilitate learning and continually assess it to guide instructional changes. Inquiry, planning, persistence, flexibility and reflection are guideposts of effective school cultures that support rigorous and individualized instruction.

Members of an effective learning community accept collective responsibility for the achievement of all students, working together to ensure that each student receives appropriate instruction and support. And all adults and students behave as if they believe that their individual and collective efforts will improve performance.

If you teach poor children and children of color at high levels, they will achieve at high levels. If you expect great things from children, they will produce great things.

Kati Haycock

Learning Centered 1

Diverse Communities 2

21st Century Learners 3

Quality Instruction 4

Knowledge and Data 5

Community Engagement 6

**Standard 2:** Reflection Questions

1. How similar or different are stakeholder descriptions of the school vision for what quality teaching and learning looks and feels like for students and adults?

2. How similar or different are student, parent, teacher and administrator descriptions of how the learning environment is meeting rigorous student learning and development needs—academic, social and physical?

3. What has to change for the school vision to represent what different stakeholders (students, parents, educators, community members) want for the education of students and what the performance data indicate is needed?

4. How are the values undergirding the school vision explicitly linked to decisions by school staff and community members about instructional practices, learning supports, administrative practices, data analysis, resource allocation and policies?

5. How can the school vision be communicated more effectively to motivate everyone to work together to attain specific student performance and development results?

6. How are relationships continuously fostered among students, families and educators from diverse cultures and economic backgrounds?

7. How accessible and diverse are the opportunities for all parents to support the learning of their children or other students?

# Standard 2: Action Steps

After answering the Reflection Questions, list the Action Steps needed to attain the learning goals specific to each question:

| Reflection Question | Action Step(s) | Who needs to take the lead? Who needs to be involved? |
|---|---|---|
| 1 | | |
| 2 | | |
| 3 | | |
| 4 | | |
| 5 | | |
| 6 | | |
| 7 | | |

1 Learning Centered
2 Diverse Communities
3 21st Century Learners
4 Quality Instruction
5 Knowledge and Data
6 Community Engagement

## Standard 2: Leadership Continuum

This self-assessment continuum is intended to help you move toward higher levels of leadership. Consider using this tool at the beginning of the school year and again at the end to assess areas of growth and to identify needed areas of personal and behavioral change.

| Strategy | Level 1 | Level 2 | Level 3 | Level 4 | Level 5 | Score Circle One |
|---|---|---|---|---|---|---|
| **1. Build consensus on a vision that reflects the core values of the school community.** | There is no explicit vision or set of beliefs guiding the work of students and adults in the school community. | There is an explicit vision often modified annually as part of a school strategic action plan to meet local, state, national or federal mandates. | The principal leads a visioning process that results in most teachers and school staff agreeing to a shared vision and core set of beliefs that help everyone understand what quality teaching and learning looks like. | The principal collaborates with some teachers, staff and stakeholders to continue leading the visioning process that results in consensus and shared ownership of a dynamic vision and a shared set of core beliefs that undergird all strategies and decisions about teaching and learning both in and out of school. | Everyone describes the school as a learning community that continuously examines the alignment of teaching and administrative practices with the school's vision, mission and core beliefs. Elements of the vision are evident in the daily language, decisions and ethical actions of almost all engaged stakeholders. | 1 2 3 4 5 |
| **2. Value and use diversity to enhance the learning of the entire school community.** | Diversity only becomes an issue when it creates dissonance with the established routines and practices of the school. Most parents from diverse backgrounds do not feel welcomed and are not involved in the school. | The principal responds to local, state, national or federal mandates to disaggregate and report student assessment scores based on demographic data and learning needs. Some parents from diverse backgrounds may be involved in formal structures as required by local, state, national or federal programs. | The principal encourages schoolwide respect and value of the backgrounds of students, and this is most often demonstrated through celebrations of holidays, historical events, field trips and guest speakers. Some teachers may take into account cultural, socio-economic backgrounds and learning needs of diverse students when creating learning experiences. The principal, teachers and a few parent leaders offer several ways for parents to be involved in the school. Many diverse parents feel comfortable in the school and offer to support athletic, social and academic events for students. | Many teachers and staff use students' diverse life experiences as the foundation for teaching and learning that engage all students in the assets of a diverse global community. Many students and family members from diverse cultures and backgrounds feel welcomed and comfortable when visiting the school and talking with teachers and administrators. The principal, teachers and parent leaders create a culture where many diverse parents feel a part of the school community and are able to support teachers and instructional experiences as well as individual student learning needs. | Students, families, administrators and teachers actively work to sustain a learning community that values diverse people, ideas, perspectives and experiences. Educators and stakeholders honor, support and value diversity as a way to increase learning, not as a barrier to learning. The principal and teachers continuously seek to engage all parents as equal partners in supporting student learning and growth. The school strategic action plan incorporates diverse parent voices, knowledge, skills and experiences to support high performance of students and adults. | 1 2 3 4 5 |

1 Learning Centered
2 Diverse Communities
3 21st Century Learners
4 Quality Instruction
5 Knowledge and Data
6 Community Engagement

| Strategy | Level 1 | Level 2 | Level 3 | Level 4 | Level 5 | Score Circle One |
|---|---|---|---|---|---|---|
| **3. Broaden the framework for child development beyond academics.** | The principal maintains a schoolwide focus on academic performance with no explicit attention to the social, emotional and physical development of the whole child. | Any focus on the development of the whole child is required by local, state, national or federal programs. Some enrichment programs may be available from individual teachers, external organizations or after-school programs. | The principal and teachers agree that a core instructional value is to develop the whole child, not just academic knowledge and skills. The principal and some teachers weave social, emotional or physical learning experiences into the curriculum. | The principal and many teachers use instructional practices designed to expand the range of student knowledge and skills in areas beyond academics, and engage students in several community programs that support the development of health, emotional, social and/or physical skills. | The principal, most teachers and some stakeholders consistently implement a balanced whole child learning culture for all students with in- and out-of-school learning experiences provided by the school and community. | 1 2 3 4 5 |
| **4. Develop a learning culture that is adaptive, collaborative, innovative and supportive.** | Annual or semester individual learning plans based on assessments exist for most special education students, but not for all students. | The principal assigns teachers to examine performance of groups of students—ELL, poverty, special education, gifted and talented—to determine annual or semester learning plans and interventions according to local, state, national or federal mandates. | The principal and some teachers discuss and pilot individual learning plans with innovative and supportive instructional practices to meet diverse student learning needs, especially for students with diverse socio-economic backgrounds and low performance. | The principal, many teachers and some staff actively work to uncover myths about diversity that are negatively influencing expectations, instructional practices and student achievement. The principal and teachers implement an adaptive system of individual learning plans for all students and adults based on formative and summative assessments and using collaborative, innovative and flexible instructional practices. | The principal, administrators, teachers, staff and some stakeholders regularly examine the implications of diverse people, ideas, perspectives and experiences in supporting increased student and adult performance. Everyone constantly examines his/her own background and experiences for biases that must change in order to better support diverse student and adult learning needs. Learning plans and instructional practices are reviewed, revised and adjusted based on performance. | 1 2 3 4 5 |

# For More Information

## On the Web

**Developmental Studies Center** (www.devstu.org) runs programs that build children's academic, ethical and social development. The site offers kits that contain resources and videos to help teachers and principals create community environments, develop programs that use cooperative structures to increase students' abilities to listen to one another and infuse academics with social skills.

**The National Art Education Association** (www.arteducators.org) promotes the inclusion of art in children's learning because of the many ways it expands children's creativity, imagination and knowledge beyond academics. Among the site's many offerings are research papers, advocacy resources, publications and links to lesson plans.

**The UCLA Center for Mental Health in Schools** (www.smhp.psych.ucla.edu) offers a Web site with free downloadable resources on mental health in education. Also available are monthly e-newsletters, networks to join and free quarterly journals.

## Resources and Research

**Annenberg Institute for School Reform. "Getting to Equity."** *Voices in Urban Education.* **No. 11. Providence, RI: Annenberg Institute for School Reform, 2006.**

This issue of *Voices in Urban Education* discusses the conversations and actions that lead to equity and excellence in achievement for all students.

**Center on Education Policy.** *Instructional Time in Elementary Schools: A Closer Look at Changes for Specific Subjects.* **Washington, D.C.: Center on Education Policy, 2008.**

This report examines the ways that the NCLB Act has changed instructional time since its enactment in 2002. It's a follow-up to the Center on Education Policy's 2007 report *Choices, Changes, and Challenges: Curriculum and Instruction in the NCLB Era.*

**Commission on the Whole Child.** *The Learning Compact Redefined: A Call to Action.* **Alexandria, VA: Association for Supervision and Curriculum Development, 2007.**

The Association for Supervision and Curriculum Development's initiative to promote a focus on the "whole child" in education is detailed in this compact. As partners, NAESP and other leading education groups are calling on communities, policymakers and educators to take action steps to address whole child education in schools.

**Chenoweth, K.** *It's Being Done: Academic Success in Unexpected Schools.* **Cambridge, MA: Harvard Education Press, 2007.**

This book explains what is effective at schools that have high rates of proficiency and trajectories of vast improvement—while also having high rates of poverty, diverse student populations or both. The author identifies 25 characteristics that are instrumental in creating and maintaining quality learning environments, or what she calls "It's Being Done" schools.

**Payne, R. K.** *A Framework for Understanding Poverty.* **Fourth edition. Highlands, TX: aha! Process Inc., 2005.**

The author presents a framework to better understand the causes of behavioral and developmental issues common to low-income children. This widely used tool is known for helping educators improve teaching methods for low-income students.

# Demand content and instruction that ensure student achievement of agreed-upon standards.

**1** Learning Centered

**2** Diverse Communities

**3** 21st Century Learners

**4** Quality Instruction

**5** Knowledge and Data

**6** Community Engagement

**W**e are living in an era that requires new thinking about our approach to educating young people. Educators and the public are shifting away from the "back to basics" mindset predominant in the 1990s to strongly supporting the idea that teaching 21st century skills is vital to our country's economic success. A recent poll by the Partnership for 21st Century Skills shows that nearly 9 in 10 voters believe that a combination of academic and more advanced "applied" skills can and should be part of school curricula.

Employers are clamoring for a better-prepared work force at a time when many high school graduates are woefully ill-equipped for a world in which being college-ready and work-ready are the same thing. Most young people enter the work force lacking the critical skills essential for success. And for those who do not graduate from high school, the chances of success are even lower.

Students in the United States need to know much more about the world than ever before. They need to know world cultures and languages, and they need high levels of knowledge and skills to thrive

The heart of instruction is the monitoring of instruction.

Dan Lortie

in an increasingly competitive and collaborative society. Skills such as global literacy, problem solving, ethics, social responsibility, teamwork, communications, innovation and creativity have joined the list of high academic skills that are critical for student success in the 21st century. Particularly in a changing economy, as economist Alan Greenspan writes in his 2007 memoir, *The Age of Turbulence: Adventures in a New World*, these skills are critical to our country's economic success.

To give students a chance at success in post-secondary education, work and citizenship, effective leaders know they have to get student learning on track even before students enter elementary school. Instructional leaders know that an early start makes it possible to reach high standards in one content area while maintaining sufficient student learning time and a balanced curriculum in others. A late start, by contrast, makes it likely that reaching high standards in one content area will mean lost learning time in others.

Leaders must adopt rigorous college-readiness standards throughout the learning continuum, from pre-K through high school, to minimize the odds that students will need remediation later. These rigorous academic standards must be the default curriculum for all students, regardless of socioeconomic background.

What does it look like when principals focus on 21st century learning? We see principals who:

- **Ensure alignment of curriculum with district and school goals, standards, assessments and resources**

- **Invest in a technology-rich culture that connects learning to the global society**

- **Hire, retain and support high-quality teachers**

- **Ensure rigorous, relevant and appropriate instruction for all students**

## Ensure alignment of curriculum with district and school goals, standards, assessments and resources

Effective instructional leaders manage more than facilities; they lead and manage the continuous improvement of instruction. Regardless of a teacher's ability, students learn more and faster every time the teacher's expectations for learning increase and his or her delivery skills are improved.

Every student must be effectively taught grade-level work every day. Research shows that the most efficient and cost-effective way to advance student learning is a schoolwide emphasis on designing and delivering lessons that help all students learn more and faster. Resources invested in tutoring, for example, help only the students who receive it. But improving the quality of all teachers has the power to benefit generations of students.

Instructional leadership means that the principal's primary day-to-day responsibility is to guide teaching throughout the building. Such a leader has a strong knowledge of what good instruction looks like, observes teachers regularly for continuous improvement feedback and evaluates them against high standards for instructional excellence. Effective leaders and teachers are knowledgeable about research on learning and engage students in purposeful learning through a relevant and rigorous curriculum. These leaders measure student time on task, alignment to standards, breadth of coverage of standards and instructional effectiveness based on student learning. Effective instructional leaders know that those four variables help to create a roadmap for learning and are indicators of productivity in classrooms.

 TERMS TO KNOW

### Learning Criteria

**Core academic learning**—Achievement in the core subjects of language arts, math, science and others identified by the school.

**Stretch learning**—Demonstration of rigorous and relevant learning beyond minimum requirements, such as participation in higher-level courses and specialized courses, and so forth.

**Student engagement**—The extent to which students are motivated and committed to learning, have a sense of belonging and accomplishment, and have relationships with adults, peers and parents that support learning.

**Personal skill development**—Measures of personal, social, service, and leadership skills and demonstrations of positive behaviors and attitudes.

Source: Daggett, W. R., and P. D. Nussbaum. "How Brain Research Relates to Rigor, Relevance and Relationships." Rexford, NY: International Center for Leadership in Education, 2007.

1 Learning Centered
2 Diverse Communities
3 21st Century Learners
4 Quality Instruction
5 Knowledge and Data
6 Community Engagement

### Invest in a technology-rich culture that connects learning to the global society

One of the most important competencies students need in the 21st century is the ability to use technology well. As young people know better than their elders, technology outside of school has transformed almost every aspect of society, from communication and recreation to the workplace. As "digital natives," young people are often more adept than their teachers (or "digital immigrants") at navigating a technological world.

The possibilities offered by new technologies suggest that learning not be limited to traditional classrooms. Effective leaders create new learning opportunities by making technology available to students. They ensure that the curriculum incorporates the kind of learning students can acquire through multimedia. And they employ assessments that measure the full range of knowledge and skills that these technologies help young people develop.

## A CLOSER LOOK

### Digital Natives and Digital Immigrants: The Disconnect Between Students and Educators

Technology has changed. So have the students sitting in classrooms across the country.

Students of the 21st century are digital learners, often referred to as "digital natives." Educators—many of whom have not changed their classroom practices to align with the 21st century world—are referred to as "digital immigrants." This translates to a disconnect between how teachers teach and how students learn.

Students today like to get information from multiple sources, and quickly. Many teachers prefer to rely on slower and more controlled methods for sharing knowledge. Students multitask, and process things in a parallel manner, while teachers tend to limit themselves to one task at a time. While teachers most often use text, students prefer pictures, sounds and videos. Students like to work in groups; yet many teachers prefer students to work independently. Students have a preference for learning about what is useful or practical, while teachers tend to focus on standards, curriculum and guidelines.

Sources: Discussion of the differences between "digital native" learners and "digital immigrant" teachers at Apple's Web site: www.apple.com/education/digitalkids/disconnect/landscape.html/

Prensky, M. "Digital Natives, Digital Immigrants." *On the Horizon,* Vol. 9, No. 5, October 2001, and at www.marcprensky.com

The explosion of multimedia, communication and information systems, along with other learning technologies, offers a myriad of avenues for student learning. Through modeling and simulations, for example, students can conduct virtual science experiments or create communities to develop their understanding of mathematics, history and geography. By creating videos, students can expand their language arts abilities by demonstrating an understanding of narrative, dialogue and other skills. Accessible technologies help students with disabilities gain access to content and people that might not be available through conventional instructional practices.

However, the digital age also requires a new set of skills, beyond the basics of using new hardware and software. Specifically, the magnitude of information the Internet has created demands an ability to consume information effectively. Students need to know not only how to gain access to information but also how to assess its quality. They need to analyze information so that they can create their own insights, not simply rely on the ideas of others.

Technology also offers the promise of enabling students to learn interactively with teachers and peers across the globe. Distance learning expands potential course offerings by enabling students to learn from experts who might not be available nearby. Interacting with peers online also enhances the diverse knowledge and perspectives students have access to, and sharpens their ability to think critically.

For example, Hellgate Intermediate School in Missoula, Montana, works as a partner with the National Aeronautics and Space Administration (NASA) in a program designed to bring NASA curriculum to educators, students and families. NASA established the program to bring together teachers and administrators from communities across the country to study science-related curriculum. In partnership with NASA, Hellgate Intermediate teachers and staff acquire and use new teaching resources and technology tools that involve NASA experts and resources.

Principals who place high value on developing students' technological literacy are often skillful information consumers themselves and can gain access to resources that enhance their own teaching and learning efforts.

Digital immigrants—teachers—are speaking an outdated language, and the digital natives—students—are speaking an entirely different one.

Marc Prensky

Learning Centered 1

Diverse Communities 2

21st Century Learners 3

Quality Instruction 4

Knowledge and Data 5

Community Engagement 6

## Hire, retain and support high-quality teachers

*What* students learn is absolutely critical; so is the quality of instruction in *how* they learn. Once 21st century standards and relevant curriculum are in place, effective instructional leaders must insist on recruiting and retaining the highest-quality teaching staff possible. Strong leaders hire strong teachers who embrace the school's vision and goals.

Hiring certified teachers is a legitimate strategy for instructional leaders, but that alone is not enough. Teachers must be willing to sustain high-quality performance throughout their careers and continually develop their professional capacities. A decade ago, the focus was setting standards and aligning the curriculum to those standards. Instructional leaders are now focused on having an aligned learning system of standards, curriculum, instruction, professional development and assessment.

This emphasis on high levels of learning for every student has shifted attention in schools and communities from *teaching* to *learning*. Assessment is critical, as students, parents and the public demand to see evidence of what students know and are able to do. No longer will it suffice for an educator to say, "I taught it, but they didn't learn it."

 A CLOSER LOOK

### 21st Century Learning Skills

Changes in technology, demographics and even politics are transforming the way we live and work every day. Schools, perhaps more than any other organization, are struggling to keep pace with this rapidly changing world. The Partnership for 21st Century Skills has proposed six key elements that will foster learning in the 21st century to better prepare students—and educators—for the ever-changing world. The partnership's vision for schools includes:

- **Emphasizing all core subjects**

- **Emphasizing learning skills, especially how to continue learning throughout life**

- **Using 21st century tools to develop learning skills, especially focused on technology**

- **Teaching and learning in a 21st century context through the use of real-world experiences**

- **Teaching and learning 21st century content, such as global awareness, and financial, economic, business and civic literacy**

- **Measuring 21st century skills using 21st century assessments that include a balance of standardized testing and classroom-based assessments**

Source: Partnership for 21st Century Skills. *Learning for the 21st Century,* Washington, D.C. : Partnership for 21st Century Skills, 2002.

# INSIDE A SCHOOL: A FOCUS ON PRACTICE

**Langston Hughes Elementary School, Baltimore, Maryland**
**Principal Gloria Pulley**

At Langston Hughes Elementary, students are given the opportunity to learn in a variety of settings that prepare them for the 21st century. Principal Gloria Pulley focuses on broadening the curriculum to enhance the experiences and lessons for her school community.

"Each month, we showcase our students on stage by having them perform what they've learned for the rest of the school, parents and the community," explains Pulley. This "academic performance" might be a schoolwide play where all students memorize lines, a short skit on the fourth grade science lessons, a published piece that a second grader wants to share or an interactive 'Jeopardy' game. Sometimes the focus of the performance is on whole child development. "We teach social skills and push character education. We did a restaurant skit where some students played elderly citizens, and the others were young, disrespectful teenagers. We are going beyond the academics here."

Creatively engaging the students has many benefits that help develop well-rounded individuals. "These performances not only provide a chance for students to think critically and learn continually, but it also helps them learn to collaborate effectively within a group and communicate with adults," adds Pulley.

Pulley also understands that one must go beyond the school doors to find useful resources for students. She's working on a partnership with a local bank to help the students learn the values of saving and investing. And she and her staff are working on offering diverse after-school programs—from art to physical fitness—that will tap the expertise in the school community and provide other avenues for students to grow and succeed.

"A combination of the academic skills, cultural enrichment and real-world experiences will help develop the whole child. We are dedicated to improving academic results and we feel strongly this is one way to do it."

1 Learning Centered
2 Diverse Communities
3 21st Century Learners
4 Quality Instruction
5 Knowledge and Data
6 Community Engagement

Everyone needs a shared vision of the benchmarks for performance—whether they are mandated from the school, district, state or federal government—and all teachers need to align their instruction to these benchmarks. Regardless of whether they support the NCLB performance criteria, effective instructional leaders must have high expectations of performance that are transparent enough that all students, parents and teachers know what targets they are aiming at. Parents of a third-grader, for example, can truly support meeting those targets only if they know what their child is expected to know and be able to do at that level.

Effective instructional leaders ensure that priorities are set for improving instruction given by every teacher, for every student. Priorities change as student and adult learning needs change and when new knowledge and skills are required of them. In addition, instructional leaders need to know how to manage a flexible school schedule that supports dynamic teaching and learning needs.

## A CLOSER LOOK

### Leading for Learning: Five Areas of Action That School and District Leaders Can Use To Advance Student Learning

Researchers at the Center for the Study of Teaching and Policy developed a set of ideas and tools for reflection that school leaders can use to improve student learning. To be successful, school leaders must engage three learning agendas—student learning, professional learning and system learning—while taking into account the influence of families, organizational conditions, and the larger policy and professional environment. To support the three learning agendas, effective school leaders should follow five action steps:

- **Establish a focus on learning by persistently and publicly focusing their own attention and that of others on learning and teaching**
- **Build professional communities that value learning by nurturing work cultures that value and support their members' learning**
- **Engage external environments for learning by building relationships and securing resources from outside groups that can foster students' or teachers' learning**
- **Act strategically and share leadership by mobilizing efforts along multiple "pathways" that lead to student, professional or system learning, and by distributing leadership across levels and among individuals in different positions**
- **Create coherence by connecting student, professional and system learning with one another and with learning goals**

Source: Knapp, M., M. Copland and J. Talbert. *Leading for Learning: Reflective Tools for School and District Leaders*. Seattle, WA: Center for the Study of Teaching and Policy, 2003.

1 Learning Centered

2 Diverse Communities

3 21st Century Learners

4 Quality Instruction

5 Knowledge and Data

6 Community Engagement

Principals have the primary responsibility to provide a range of resources to teachers—from lesson plans to learning materials, assessments and professional development opportunities—to expand their pedagogical skills and toolboxes. A growing number of organizations, in the United States and other countries, are developing tools for teachers, and many are available over the Internet. As principals expand their face-to-face and electronic networks, they learn about new tools and information for their faculties. Community organizations can also be important resources, and cultural organizations can help teachers understand pedagogical approaches for students from diverse backgrounds.

In addition, in the view of Kate Walsh, the president of the National Council on Teacher Quality, leadership is the key issue when it comes to teachers' working conditions. She rejects the idea that teachers leave their jobs just because a school has a high number of low-income children. Effective and supportive leadership also crops up consistently as the single most important issue in the working conditions surveys that the Center on Teaching Quality has helped conduct in Arizona, Kansas, Mississippi, Nevada, North Carolina, Ohio and South Carolina.

Good teachers will not work for bad principals.

Barnett Berry

## INSIDE A SCHOOL: A FOCUS ON PRACTICE

**Blythewood Middle School, Blythewood, South Carolina**
**Principal Nancy Gregory**

A few years ago Blythewood Middle School began a new program to incorporate technology into the classroom. Principal Nancy Gregory, along with a social studies teacher and a language arts teacher, set up a shared classroom space filled with computers and portable labs, divided by an accordion wall. Gregory worked out a block schedule for the two teachers, enabling them to share a group of students. The set-up allows the teachers to team-teach or flip-flop classrooms, and provides more flexibility for students, giving those who may need it, more time on task. "It gives the teacher the ability to differentiate, because we know that some kids need more time," says Gregory.

The classrooms are equipped with SMART Board technology and Discovery Education Unitedstreaming, a digital video-based learning resource. Students have access to Blackboard for homework assignments, using a data drop box to submit completed assignments to teachers. Students can also talk to a teacher from home when they are preparing for a test—a big plus for both students and teachers, says Gregory. "You can give immediate feedback to the kids to help with your teaching, knowing when to adjust," she notes.

The pay-off has been the teachers' ability to engage the students—often a difficult task with middle-school-aged students. "It is so appealing to them, it makes learning fun and interesting," says Gregory.

Supported by a "tech savvy" superintendent, Gregory has been able to expand the program. What started in one classroom has now expanded to grades 6, 7 and 8, with teachers from other disciplines clamoring to join in.

## Ensure rigorous, relevant and appropriate instruction for all students

In his influential and best-selling 2005 book, *The World Is Flat: A Brief History of the Twenty-First Century*, journalist Thomas L. Friedman showed how the spread of fiber-optic cable throughout the world transformed the global economy and society. Once telecommunications became ubiquitous, countries such as China and India could compete on the world stage in a way that was not possible before. As Americans are increasingly aware, the person at the call center is as likely to be in Delhi as in Denver; the accountant preparing taxes might be in Shanghai rather than Springfield.

As a result, students in the United States need to know much more about the world than ever before. They need to know world cultures and languages to be able to collaborate effectively with business partners halfway around the globe, and they need high levels of knowledge and skills to thrive in an increasingly competitive and collaborative society.

Effective leaders know that while schools do not control all of the factors that shape students' motivation to learn, rigorous and relevant instruction can be structured in a way that significantly influences attitudes and behavior. In addition to ensuring that instruction is relevant to students, effective leaders foster instruction that is relevant to society.

In his paper, "Preparing Students for Their Future," Willard Daggett, president of the International Center for Leadership in Education, identifies four "mega trends" that must be addressed to ensure that our nation and our students are prepared to meet the challenges of the near and distant future. These four challenges are globalization, changing demographics, technology, and changing values and attitudes. "We are finding it easy to conceptualize change," Daggett writes, "but difficult to implement it. Tinkering at the margins will not enable us to achieve our mission. Schools need to be restructured if they are serious about getting all students to the high standards necessary for them to compete and excel in the global society."

1 Learning Centered

2 Diverse Communities

3 21st Century Learners

4 Quality Instruction

5 Knowledge and Data

6 Community Engagement

## A CLOSER LOOK

### Rigor/Relevance Framework™

Educators can use the Rigor/Relevance Framework to create learning experiences that engage students in real-world applications. To find out more about the Framework, visit: www.leadered.com/rigor.html.

| KNOWLEDGE | | APPLICATION | | | |
|---|---|---|---|---|---|
| Evaluation 6 | | | | | |
| Synthesis 5 | **ASSIMILATION** **C** | | **ADAPTATION** **D** | | |
| Analysis 4 | | | | | |
| Application 3 | | | | | |
| Comprehension 2 | **ACQUISITION** **A** | | **APPLICATION** **B** | | |
| Awareness 1 | | | | | |
| | **1** Knowledge in one discipline | **2** Apply knowledge in one discipline | **3** Apply knowledge across disciplines | **4** Apply knowledge to real-world predictable situations | **5** Apply knowledge to real-world unpredictable situations |

**APPLICATION**

Source: International Center for Leadership in Education (www.leadered.com).

To help education leaders align curriculum, instruction and assessment to meet these challenges, the International Center has designed the Rigor/Relevance Framework. The framework supports the use of instructional strategies designed to maximize mental stimulation and cooperative learning instead of isolated, rote memorization of facts. Rather than use lectures and other traditional instructional techniques, the Center encourages educators to employ strategies that engage students and treat them as active learners rather than empty receptacles into which knowledge can be poured. By doing so, schools become a place where students work and teachers observe, not the other way around.

Current brain research suggests that rather than being sedentary, passive and aligned in neat rows of desks, learners should be allowed to be tactile, experiential, interactive and social and to move purposefully around the classroom as part of the learning process. Active learning provides multisensory stimuli to the brain.

In addition, effective leaders abandon the practice known as ability "tracking," in which students of similar achievement levels are always taught together. The research is clear: Tracking isolates low-performing or unmotivated students and results in lower teacher expectations, remedial instruction, slower social development, lower performance results and the creation of a lock-stepped, slower-paced instruction that is neither relevant nor rigorous. Simply put, just because students have similar academic performances or learning needs does not mean they can all be taught the same way.

Schools that successfully engage students in learning have a number of things in common: They set high academic standards and provide rigorous, meaningful instruction and support so that all students can meet them. Effective school structures make it possible to give students individual attention. Teachers take an interest in students' lives, drawing on children's real-world experiences and current understandings to build new knowledge. Adults show students the connections between success in school and achieving long-term career plans.

## define TERMS TO KNOW

### Soft Skills

Personal qualities

- Responsibility

- Integrity

- Ethics

Interpersonal skills

- Communicate effectively

- Work well with others in a diverse and collaborative environment

- Lead work of diverse groups

Source: The Partnership for 21st Century Skills. *Learning for the 21st Century.* Washington, D.C.: The Partnership for 21st Century Skills, 2003.

1 Learning Centered
2 Diverse Communities
3 21st Century Learners
4 Quality Instruction
5 Knowledge and Data
6 Community Engagement

**Standard 3:** Reflection Questions

1. Are the standards, curriculum, learning experiences, professional development and assessments aligned to district and school goals?

2. What adult expectations for student learning and development need to be raised to improve student performance and meet learning needs of all students?

3. What student learning is showing increased performance over time?

4. How can learning experiences better prepare students to be global citizens and succeed in a global workplace?

5. How can a wide range of learning experiences be offered that support student development of knowledge and skills beyond mandated testing?

6. How can the learning culture be enriched with technology so that it supports application of skills?

7. How can students become more skillful synthesizers and consumers of information, given the immediate access they have to varied and complex information from worldwide sources?

8. Why do high-quality teachers say they do or do not want to continue teaching at this school?

9. What programs, teaching strategies, assessment measures or learning experiences need to be revised or eliminated because they are ineffective in supporting student or adult learning?

10. How can effective pilot teaching and learning efforts go to scale so all students benefit from the effective practices?

# Standard 3: Action Steps

After answering the Reflection Questions, list the Action Steps needed to attain the learning goals specific to each question:

| Reflection Question | Action Step(s) | Who needs to take the lead? Who needs to be involved? |
|---|---|---|
| 1 | | |
| 2 | | |
| 3 | | |
| 4 | | |
| 5 | | |
| 6 | | |
| 7 | | |
| 8 | | |
| 9 | | |
| 10 | | |

1 Learning Centered

2 Diverse Communities

3 21st Century Learners

4 Quality Instruction

5 Knowledge and Data

6 Community Engagement

# Standard 3: Leadership Continuum

This self-assessment continuum is intended to help you move toward higher levels of leadership. Consider using this tool at the beginning of the school year and again at the end to assess areas of growth and to identify needed areas of personal and behavioral change.

| Strategy | Level 1 | Level 2 | Level 3 | Level 4 | Level 5 | Score Circle One |
|---|---|---|---|---|---|---|
| **1. Ensure alignment of curriculum with district and school goals, standards, assessments and resources.** | School curriculum matches district goals and expectations, standards and assessments. Principal distributes resources and teachers augment them when necessary. | Some realignment of school expectations, standards, curriculum, assessments and allocation of resources may occur to accommodate local, state, national or federal mandates that are not districtwide. | The principal facilitates a process with teachers to create a unique identity for the school and establish school goals designed to meet the specific learning needs of the student population. The process includes an intentional review of the entire curriculum, standards, range of assessments and allocation of resources to determine needed revision or expansion. | The principal combines an ongoing visioning process with establishment of school goals based on consensus of core teaching and learning values that determine the standards, curriculum, assessments and allocation of resources. School learning communities examine and align school and district goals, standards and curriculum. The principal and many teachers set explicit and measurable high expectations for themselves and most students. | The principal, teachers and community partners revisit school goals based on changing school community demographics and community expectations for results. The school curriculum is repeatedly examined to ensure growth, refinement, realignment and new standards because of rapid advances in knowledge about how people learn and how to measure learning. Everyone raises expectations for their learning and performance. | 1 2 3 4 5 |

| Strategy | Level 1 | Level 2 | Level 3 | Level 4 | Level 5 | Score Circle One |
|---|---|---|---|---|---|---|
| **2. Invest in a technology-rich culture that connects learning to the global society.** | The principal determines the level of investment in technology to support student learning and performance. Technology is regarded as an administrative, record-keeping and communication investment.<br><br>A few teachers may use technology, but instruction that engages students in using varied technologies to increase learning does not exist throughout the school, and there are no schoolwide efforts to ensure that students are media literate. | Instruction that engages students in using varied technologies to increase learning or to ensure that students become media-literate, skillful synthesizers and consumers of information is limited to what is required by local, state, national or federal mandates. | The principal or some teachers actively engage students in using a few technologies primarily to develop specific skill sets or to create learning products.<br><br>There is limited school investment in multiple technologies, professional development for effective teaching and learning practices, and learning experiences to promote media literacy. | The principal, teachers, and some students and stakeholders are involved in developing a school plan to use varied technologies to support student and adult learning and performance.<br><br>The principal and many teachers engage most students in using various media to become skilled consumers and synthesizers of information, data and resource gatherers, and creators of products, as well as becoming media-literate virtual learners. | The principal, teachers, students and stakeholders work together to ensure the use of 21st century technology tools to access information, communicate, learn and produce work.<br><br>The school community is a learning environment in which the global society is made real through the investment in and infusion of digital learning for students and adults. | 1<br>2<br>3<br>4<br>5 |
| **3. Hire, retain and support high-quality teachers.** | District hiring procedures are followed and there is no formal schoolwide focus on retaining and supporting high-quality teachers. | Hiring, retention and support efforts for high-quality teachers satisfy district guidelines and any legal or unique requirements by local, state, national or federal mandates. | The principal and teacher leaders informally recruit high-quality teachers and analyze disaggregated student performance data to determine high-quality teachers on whom support and retention efforts should be focused. | The principal and many teachers develop a marketing plan based on the school learning culture to recruit high-quality teachers.<br><br>With a comprehensive development plan and focused allocation of resources, all teachers are expected to improve. | The principal, teachers and stakeholders are engaged in determining how to recruit, celebrate, support and retain high-quality teachers.<br><br>Everyone finds new resources to support creative professional development opportunities. | 1<br>2<br>3<br>4<br>5 |
| **4. Ensure rigorous, relevant and appropriate instruction for all students.** | Definitions of rigor and relevance are individual teacher decisions. Differentiated instruction rarely occurs. Appropriateness is measured by grade level or an individual education plan. | Rigor, relevance and appropriate instruction are defined by the district and individual teachers. Variance may occur based on requirements of local, state, national and federal programs.<br><br>There are limited, if any, applied learning partnerships with universities, businesses and community organizations. | The principal and some teachers often consider and implement specific high-quality research-based instructional practices, but generally these rigorous practices are teacher- or program-driven and may not be schoolwide.<br><br>The principal and a few teachers involve students in periodic real-world, topic-based, nonrecurring events through varied partnerships. | The principal and most teachers regularly implement rigorous curriculum and differentiated instruction for all students, and regularly embed real-world learning experiences for most students.<br><br>Partnerships often expand applied learning to community-based and virtual experiences. | The principal, all teachers and many community leaders expect rigorous experiential learning and development for all students.<br><br>Networks are constantly explored for sustainable community partnerships to support real-world learning and developmental needs of individual students. | 1<br>2<br>3<br>4<br>5 |

1 Learning Centered
2 Diverse Communities
3 21st Century Learners
4 Quality Instruction
5 Knowledge and Data
6 Community Engagement

# For More Information

## On the Web

**The Association for Supervision and Curriculum Development** (www.ascd.org) offers articles, books, videos and other online tools that share best practices and sound policies in education. Materials on professional development, field networks and effective advocacy are available at this site.

**The Center for Teaching Quality** (www.teachingquality.org) advances the profession through developing teacher leadership, conducting practical research and engaging various communities. The site offers resources on redefining the teacher as a leader, evaluating working conditions, teacher preparation and mentoring.

**The Consortium for School Networking** (www.cosn.org) provides products and services that support leadership development, advocacy, coalition building and awareness of emerging technologies. The site provides free education technology resources and information on leadership initiatives to improve technology in K-12 schools.

**The International Society for Technology in Education** (www.iste.org) works to provide knowledge, leadership and service to improve teaching, learning and school leadership by advancing effective uses of technology in PK-12 education. Included among the many offerings on the site are free educational resources and a host of links to online software that promotes the use of technology in curriculum, standards assessments and student-driven goal setting.

**The National Comprehensive Center for Teacher Quality** (www.ncctq.org) provides information on how to strengthen schools with quality teaching. The site offers free online resources, publications and Web casts that address teacher preparation, teacher recruitment and retention and teaching in at-risk schools.

## Resources and Research

**The Center for Comprehensive School Reform and Improvement. "Using the Classroom Walk-Through as an Instructional Leadership Strategy." Washington, D.C. : The Center for Comprehensive School Reform and Improvement, 2007.**

This article describes the essential elements of an effective classroom walkthrough as a tool for instructional supervision.

**Partnership for 21st Century Skills. "Beyond the Three Rs: Voter Attitudes Toward 21st Century Skills." Tucson, AZ: Partnership for 21st Century Skills, 2007.**

This report summarizes a poll conducted by Public Opinion Strategies and Peter D. Hart Research Associates about how the United States is preparing children for the 21st century. Registered voters reveal that Americans are concerned with young people's abilities to compete in an increasingly global economy.

**Schmoker, M. *Results Now: How We Can Achieve Unprecedented Improvements in Teaching and Learning.* Alexandria, VA: Association for Supervision and Curriculum Development (ASCD), 2006.**

The author uses research evidence, case studies and anecdotes from a variety of schools to identify the most pervasive obstacles to school improvement. Learn how a school can exceed expectations, swiftly reduce achievement gaps and enhance the lifetime learning of all students by concentrating on what really counts.

# Create a culture of continuous learning for adults tied to student learning and other school goals.

1 Learning Centered
2 Diverse Communities
3 21st Century Learners
4 Quality Instruction
5 Knowledge and Data
6 Community Engagement

**M**any principals are finding that, as organizations, schools are not designed to respond to the pressure for performance that standards and accountability bring. At the same time, effective leaders know that they need to translate this pressure for performance into meaningful work for students and adults. This means leaders must move away from the traditional structures and practices of schools, while at the same time not push teachers, who may never have been trained for this new work culture, too hard. Particularly for educators working in learning environments marked by extreme poverty and increased diversity, new levels of knowledge and skill are required.

In addition, effective leaders know that they need to build structures and supports that enable teachers to work and learn together, around relevant and timely issues. But, for the most part, teachers still operate under conditions that severely limit their exposure to other adults doing the same work. Richard Elmore of the Harvard

Improvement takes recognition of and moral outrage at ineffective practices.

Roland Barth

INSIDE A SCHOOL: A FOCUS ON PRACTICE

**Garfield Elementary School, Mentor, Ohio**
**Principal Ken Buckley**

As a 41-year veteran in education, Ken Buckley has learned that schools work better for students when teachers work together. Every day Buckley gathers his teachers to pore over research and analyze student achievement data, broken down by demographic groups, and to discuss possible solutions.

"Operating in isolation is not the best way to go," he says. "All of us have talents and strengths. If we share them, that enhances learning for everyone."

To carve out time for teacher learning, Buckley has structured the school day so that all teachers are free to meet while students take classes in art, music, physical education or media. He also has obtained waivers from the state to provide his school with pupil-free days for professional development for teachers.

To Buckley, professional development is an obligation. "It's my responsibility," he says. "Every morning, I read professional journals before I go to work." He also teaches workshops, which requires him to stay on top of the literature.

Buckley's attention to professional learning for his entire staff has paid off for Garfield. Three years ago, when he first became principal, the school's test scores had been sagging. But they have been going up each year, and in 2007, the school was rated "Excellent."

Buckley attributes some of the success to the school's dedication to improving achievement for every student. He is a strong believer in using data to drive decisions, and his teacher groups look at state test results to figure out "tiered" strategies for all students—those who need remediation as well as those who are performing at the highest levels. That's an important consideration for a school that includes students from expensive homes as well as students lower-income neighborhoods. "I'm always interested in what we can do to meet everyone's needs," he says.

Graduate School of Education writes, "The prevailing assumption is that teachers learn most of what they need to know about how to teach before they enter the classroom—despite massive evidence to the contrary." Furthermore, once they are employed in schools, teachers' professional development courses may be totally unconnected to their daily work.

Larger expectations for teachers create an extraordinary demand on school leaders, who know that the learning of adults is a prerequisite to the learning of children. With the advent of performance-based accountability, many schools have embraced the link between student achievement and teaching quality, advocating for relevant and improved staff development. The urgency now for school leaders is to plan and implement high-quality staff development—schoolwide as well as for individuals—and to create the kind of powerful professional learning that will transform teaching so that it increases learning for students.

Effective leaders create learning communities within schools that ensure that adults have many opportunities to work and learn together—whether sharing ideas and knowledge, developing and testing new approaches, or studying and analyzing student performance data.

What does it look like when principals lead a culture of continuous learning for adults? We see principals who:

- **Invest in comprehensive professional development for all adults to support student learning**

- **Align the schoolwide professional development plan with school and learning goals**

- **Encourage adults to broaden networks to bring new knowledge and resources to learning environments**

- **Provide time, structures and opportunities for adults to plan, work, reflect and celebrate together to improve practice**

The most promising strategy for sustained, substantive school improvement is building the capacity of school personnel to function as a professional learning community.

Milbrey McLaughlin

1 Learning Centered

2 Diverse Communities

3 21st Century Learners

4 Quality Instruction

5 Knowledge and Data

6 Community Engagement

## Invest in comprehensive professional development for all adults to support student learning

Effective leaders who hold teachers accountable for performance know that they, in turn, must invest in the capacity and skills of teachers. Because many teachers did not come into high-performing school cultures with the knowledge and experience to manage systems of accountability or analyze various metrics of student performance, they have to learn to do their work differently and find new ways to collaborate. By supporting teachers' growth and collaboration, principals do more than improve performance in the short term; they build the trust and accountability that can hold learning communities together.

Effective leaders invest in continuous learning through professional development at four levels:

- **School learning.** In years past, schoolwide professional development generally was concentrated at the beginning of the school year. Essentially motivational and informational, it was seldom aligned with a comprehensive schoolwide professional development plan based on student and adult learning needs. Relevant, flexible and results-based professional development is now offered throughout the year, allowing adult learning to be more aligned to student learning needs as they arise.

- **Administrator learning.** Principals need continual professional development to build leadership capacity to communicate knowledgeably and successfully with teachers and other adults about teaching, and to implement learning practices and available resources that will be most effective for student and adult learning. Key learning areas for principals are leading and managing organizational change, creating and managing student and adult accountability systems, and mentoring and coaching.

- **Teacher learning.** Effective leaders expect and invest in continual professional development to support both individual and group learning needs of teachers and other adults. Providing rigorous and relevant content, analyzing data, reflecting on teaching practice, implementing action research (studying what's happening in the school) and participating in learning communities both in and out of school are key areas of essential learning.

- **Student learning.** Ultimately, adult learning must be reflected in the advanced performance of all students. Using learning communities to identify learning needs of individuals and groups of students provides a basis for focused professional development that results in narrowing achievement gaps and raising the level of achievement for all students. Students profit most when all adults work together to effectively support learning. To do this, teachers and other adults must be involved in professional development that enhances their ability to engage with students, parents and families.

# INSIDE A SCHOOL: A FOCUS ON PRACTICE

### Centre Ridge Elementary School, Centreville, Virginia
### Principal Jim Baldwin

The NCLB Act was a wake-up call for Centre Ridge Elementary, prompting more focused attention on the individual student needs once it became clear that not *all* student subgroups were achieving. "We found that we needed to drill down to look at each child to say what we could do to make this child more successful," says Principal Jim Baldwin.

Baldwin—along with a veteran staff—has put in motion a number of strategies for creating a strong focus on learning at the school. The master schedule was adjusted to set a common planning time for teachers to meet by grade level. By scheduling an entire grade level of students into art, physical education and music, teachers were able to meet as a group at least a few times a week to discuss instructional strategies.

The structure of the day was examined to create time for teachers to teach, reteach and to enrich, says Baldwin. The school uses an approach they call SET, or student enhancement time, which sets aside time at the end of the day for a teacher to reteach a concept to students who did not grasp it, enrich the activities for those students who did or give students more time to practice what they learned.

Block scheduling for language arts and math was also introduced to allow more focused time on those subjects. Staffing assignments were also adjusted to more effectively assign staff to high-need areas.

One result, says Baldwin, is that students are more engaged in the learning process. "The children get excited about doing things and showing how well they can do," he says.

1 Learning Centered

2 Diverse Communities

3 21st Century Learners

4 Quality Instruction

5 Knowledge and Data

6 Community Engagement

Effective leaders also find ways to invest in and embed technology to support continuous learning for all adults. Systems now exist to support around-the-clock professional development learning opportunities beyond the school community. School leaders weave a range of technologies to support increased learning opportunities for individual and collective learning. E-mail has made the flow of information easier within schools, allowing faculty and team meetings to be more focused on collaborative efforts. Teachers are taking more online courses; blogs, vlogs (video blogs), content and lesson plan Web sites, and podcasts are being used more extensively. Webinars (meetings or presentations via the Internet) allow groups or teams of teachers and administrators to get information quickly, particularly in situations where states or districts can share updates on regulations, administrative issues and/or specific training on a teaching tool, curriculum product or lesson plan. Audio and video conference calls allow teachers and principals to talk to their counterparts in other schools and discuss and demonstrate effective teaching practices.

 A CLOSER LOOK

### Five Minds for the Future

We live in a fast-paced society, with constant change in technology and a wealth of data and information at our fingertips. While much attention is focused on how to prepare students, and even teachers, for the 21st century, a leading researcher in cognition has proposed ideas for how to prepare *leaders* for the 21st century. Howard Gardner, senior director of Harvard's Project Zero, suggests that leaders will need to possess five cognitive abilities to succeed in the future. The abilities, including Gardner's definitions, are:

- **The Disciplinary Mind**—The mastery of major schools of thought, including science, mathematics and history, and of at least one professional craft

- **The Synthesizing Mind**—The ability to integrate ideas from different disciplines or spheres into a coherent whole and to communicate that integration to others

- **The Creating Mind**—The capacity to uncover and clarify new problems, questions and phenomena

- **The Respectful Mind**—Awareness of and appreciation for differences among human beings and human groups

- **The Ethical Mind**—Fulfillment of one's responsibilities as a worker and citizen

Source: Gardner, H. *Five Minds for the Future*. Boston: Harvard Business School Press, 2007.

1 Learning Centered

2 Diverse Communities

3 21st Century Learners

4 Quality Instruction

5 Knowledge and Data

6 Community Engagement

### Align the schoolwide professional development plan with school and learning goals

Whether mandated or financed by the school, district or state, effective leaders work to align every teacher, administrator or team professional development experience to the school vision and students' learning needs. If, for example, the school is focused on literacy development, then professional development needs to be focused on pedagogy and resources that can support learning of literacy in ways that raise performance. Effective leaders know that new approaches may be needed to move the school from previous efforts that have failed to raise performance for all students.

When school populations change—for instance, when a school gets a significant influx of students from diverse backgrounds, special education students or students from a merger with another school's English language learner program—effective school leaders require all adults to have high expectations for the improved achievement of underperforming students. In addition, effective leaders immediately provide support for all adults in the school to learn state-of-the-art practices to meet the learning needs of new students.

Effective leaders insist that teachers who attend professional development workshops, trainings and conferences be laser-focused on what those sessions will do to improve the learning of students and adults in their schools. Because teachers are learning on behalf of the entire school community, before teachers participate in professional development they are expected to create a plan for what they or other adults in the school need to learn. When teachers return to school, effective leaders create space and time for teachers to bring their learning into the school and discuss with other adults the implications for changes in administrative or instructional practices.

## A CLOSER LOOK

### Best Practice Framework

The Best Practice Framework provides a method for exploring and examining the practices of high-performing schools as compared to those of average-performing ones. Visiting the Framework online that is displayed below allows principals to deeply examine different practices, learn the critical attributes of the high-performing schools and read case studies about the many schools studied. For more information, visit: www.just4kids.org/en/research_policy/best_practices/framework.cfm

| | | | |
|---|---|---|---|
| **Recognition, Intervention and Adjustment** | Recognize, intervene or adjust based on school performance | Recognize, intervene or adjust based on teacher performance | Recognize, intervene or adjust based on student performance |
| **Monitoring: Compilation, Analysis and Use of Data** | Develop student assessment and data monitoring systems to monitor school performance | Monitor teacher performance and student learning | Monitor student learning |
| **Instructional Programs, Practices and Arrangements** | Provide evidence-based instructional programs | Ensure the use of evidence-based programs, practices and arrangements in every classroom | Use evidence-based programs, practices and arrangements |
| **Staff Selection, Leadership and Capacity Building** | Provide strong leaders, highly qualified teachers and aligned professional development | Select, develop and allocate staff based on student learning | Collaborate in grade level/ subject teams focused on student learning |
| **Student Learning: Expectations and Goals** | Provide clear, prioritized academic objectives by grade and subject that all students are expected to master | Implement the district's written curriculum and ensure that all students achieve specific academic goals | Ensure the district's written curriculum is taught to and mastered by all students |
| | **District** | **School** | **Classroom** |

Source: National Center for Educational Achievement, Just for the Kids (www.just4kids.org).

## Encourage adults to broaden networks to bring new knowledge and resources to learning environments

Learning communities extend beyond a single school or district, and effective leaders consider principals and teachers from high-performing schools to be important resources. By forming networks with other schools, school leaders enable everyone in the learning community to share ideas and tools that help fulfill the school's vision for effective student learning. These networks can be informal or formal, with regular meeting times; principals can also set up virtual discussions with colleagues from other schools.

Learning networks can also include community members who share knowledge and resources. An English language arts network, for example, might include faculty from a local university or a librarian; a science network might include staff from a natural history museum or hospital. The Internet expands the potential membership exponentially.

Networks serve a variety of functions. Principals and other school staff discuss common problems with peers, perhaps collaborating to solve problems in real time. And they can serve as working groups to enable principals and their peers from other schools and institutions to engage in deep dialogues about instructional issues and collaboratively develop products, such as formative assessment tools.

Many educators benefit from participation in regional or national subject-matter networks or school reform consortia that connect schools with common interests. While most such networks have face-to-face meetings, increasing numbers of participants use electronic means such as e-mail, Listservs and bulletin boards to communicate between meetings or as a substitute for meetings. Such virtual networks can provide important sources of information and knowledge as well as the interpersonal support required to persist over time in changing complex schoolwide or classroom practices.

In addition, teachers are getting students into learning networks. More students at all performance levels—not just gifted and talented students—are networking in local, state, national and international academic competitions or project-based learning. And they're going beyond the traditional Odyssey of the Mind or spelling bee competitions. For instance,

A successful face-to-face team is more than just collectively intelligent. It makes everyone work harder, think smarter and reach better conclusions than they would have on their own.

James Surowiecki

1 Learning Centered

2 Diverse Communities

3 21st Century Learners

4 Quality Instruction

5 Knowledge and Data

6 Community Engagement

Brevard County, Florida, offers FIRST Robotics to all high schools, and has moved the program into the middle and elementary levels, where students are building global networks relevant to 21st century work. The program also widens students' networks locally by bringing students from parochial and private schools into the learning community.

Networks are particularly important for new principals, who need mentors to guide them through their first years. But mentors can be effective only if they are appropriately trained. The Peer Assisted Leadership Services (PALS) Corps, created by NAESP and Nova Southeastern University, enables mentors to develop the skills to effectively support novice principals; the program provides the only national mentor certification in the United States. Supported by universities and professional associations, the use of mentors during the critical first few years of being an administrator and coaching for continuous leadership development is growing rapidly.

 A CLOSER LOOK

### The Importance of Mentoring

Educators are well aware of the growing shortage of qualified, effective candidates for principal positions and the challenge of retaining highly experienced principals. Federal and state legislative mandates are placing greater burdens of accountability on school principals and requiring the development of mentoring programs for principals. In addition, the fact that principals are leading increasingly diverse communities of learners has posed new challenges to the job. The profession of principal-to-principal mentoring is evolving in response to these changes.

NAESP, in partnership with Nova Southeastern University, has developed a national principal mentoring certification program. Through the Peer Assisted Leadership Services (PALS) Corps, principals have professional support, ongoing growth opportunities and rigorous training throughout their careers. A large focus of the PALS Corps addresses the changing landscape of educational leadership, particularly with regard to cultural competence and what it means to lead a diverse community. With and through mentoring, principals discover how they value diversity and learn ways to adapt themselves and their staffs to better understand different cultures and the learning needs of all students.

Source: National Association of Elementary School Principals PALS Corps (go to www.naesp.org and click Professional Development).

## Provide time, structures and opportunities for adults to plan, work, reflect and celebrate together to improve practice

Staff development that has as its goal high levels of learning for all students, teachers and administrators requires a form of professional learning quite different from the traditional workshop-driven approach. According to the National Staff Development Council, the most powerful forms of staff development occur in ongoing learning communities or teams that meet on a regular basis, preferably several times a week, for the purposes of sharing knowledge, joint lesson planning and problem solving. Effective leaders, expecting a commitment to results-based continuous improvement and innovation, support these teams by training them in the use of effective meeting processes and collaborative work tools.

Effective leaders engage in deep dialogue about teaching practices and keep their learning communities focused on learning needs they have not yet successfully addressed. They structure faculty meetings that enable a shift from information sharing to substantive dialogue about pedagogy and ways to support learning. They work across the entire learning community to look at data to assess teaching effectiveness, to ensure that adults, as well as students, are continually learning.

 **TERMS TO KNOW**

### Professional Learning Community

The term "professional learning community" is often used by educators, school leaders and administrators. Yet too often it is a catch-all phrase for activities that lose sight of the core principles of professional learning communities. Here are three ideas to keep in mind when thinking about professional learning communities:

- **Ensuring that students learn.** The professional learning community model assumes that the mission of schools is not simply to ensure that students are taught, but to ensure that they *learn*. This is a distinct shift from a focus on teaching to a focus on learning.

- **A culture of collaboration.** Educators who are building a professional learning community should work collaboratively to achieve the goal of learning for all.

- **A focus on results.** Professional learning communities should be based on results. Improving student achievement is an ongoing process that involves identifying the current level of student achievement, establishing a goal to improve the current level, working collaboratively to achieve the goal and showing evidence of progress.

Source: DuFour, R. "What Is a 'Professional Learning Community'?" *Educational Leadership.* Vol. 61, No. 8. Alexandria, VA: Association for Supervision and Curriculum Development, 2004.

Learning Centered 1
Diverse Communities 2
21st Century Learners 3
Quality Instruction 4
Knowledge and Data 5
Community Engagement 6

## INSIDE A SCHOOL: A FOCUS ON PRACTICE

**North Fairview Elementary School, Topeka, Kansas**
**Principal Edward Albert**

The motto of North Fairview Elementary School is "Spreading our wings; reaching new heights," and Edward Albert and the school team have developed a range of approaches to help students do just that.

One initiative was to harness the power of technology to support student learning. When Albert arrived at the school in the early 1990s, North Fairview had only one computer. By 1995, North Fairview had the first elementary school computer lab in the district.

But the school's goal was to integrate technology in learning, not to divert students from the content. So he adopted programs known as Accelerated Reader and Accelerated Math, which provide students with opportunities to explore learning on their own, with the teacher as a guide. The school has also invested in "clickers," which provide teachers with real-time feedback on student understanding. "Children are leaving here feeling they truly are learners," Albert says.

But learning technology is not the only innovative solution Albert and his team have implemented. They also recognized that learning requires students to feel nurtured and safe. So they divided the school into "families," which connect students across grade levels with one another and with an adult, either a teacher or paraprofessional. Now known as "Accelerated Learning Families" ("ALFs"), the groups consist of students in grades two through six and an adult. "It's a powerful way to connect students to each other," Albert says. And he should know: He led an ALF himself. "We had a great time," he says. "I got a chance to hang out with the kids."

Effective learning communities create action research projects around the effectiveness of teaching to meet students' learning needs and to identify underperforming students and groups of students. Action research is the study of what's happening in the school—through the collection and use of data—to make it a better place. It requires a plan of action, research, collection of data, testing new approaches, study of results and decisions about future actions. In addition to action research projects, some members of the school faculty serve on school improvement teams or committees that focus on the goals and methods of schoolwide and district improvement.

Administrators convene regular meetings of learning communities to deepen understanding of instructional leadership, identify practical ways to assist teachers in improving the quality of student work, critique one another's school improvement efforts, benchmark effective leadership practices and learn important skills such as how to analyze data and provide helpful feedback to teachers.

Effective leaders establish flexible schedules to support collaborative professional development structures of teachers, staff and stakeholders working together to help each other in pursuit of new knowledge and skills. Everyone celebrates progress as the school's vision is implemented.

As Elmore of Harvard writes, "The existing structure and culture of schools seems better designed to resist learning and improvement than to enable it. ...There are few portals through which new knowledge about teaching and learning can enter schools; few structures or processes in which teachers and administrators can assimilate, adapt and polish new ideas and practices; and few sources of assistance for those who are struggling to understand the connection between the academic performance of their students and the practices in which they engage."

Providing the time, structures and opportunities for continuous learning is a central challenge for effective school leaders.

1 Learning Centered

2 Diverse Communities

3 21st Century Learners

4 Quality Instruction

5 Knowledge and Data

6 Community Engagement

# **?** | Standard 4: Reflection Questions

1. How can investments in professional development for improving teaching and learning increase the use of effective practices and provide continuous learning experiences for all teachers throughout the year?

2. What shared understanding exists among teachers, administrators, students, parents and community members about what quality teaching and learning looks and feels like?

3. How can teaching practices and learning experiences more effectively engage diverse people, ideas, perspectives and experiences?

4. What collaborative structures, resource supports and tools can most effectively support an adult learning culture that results in changed expectations and practices that increase student and adult learning?

5. What evidence is there that the investment in professional development is changing teaching practices that result in increased student learning?

6. How can teachers examine student work in ways that illuminate effective and ineffective teaching practices and result in changes to more effective practices by all teachers?

7. How can adults observe, assess, showcase and celebrate effective teaching that engages all students in rigorous learning?

8. What effective teaching and learning practices within the school, district, state, nation or world could address student learning needs currently not being met?

# Standard 4: Action Steps

After answering the Reflection Questions, list the Action Steps needed to attain the learning goals specific to each question:

| Reflection Question | Action Step(s) | Who needs to take the lead? Who needs to be involved? |
|---|---|---|
| 1 | | |
| 2 | | |
| 3 | | |
| 4 | | |
| 5 | | |
| 6 | | |
| 7 | | |
| 8 | | |

1 Learning Centered

2 Diverse Communities

3 21st Century Learners

4 Quality Instruction

5 Knowledge and Data

6 Community Engagement

## Standard 4: Leadership Continuum

This self-assessment continuum is intended to help you move toward higher levels of leadership. Consider using this tool at the beginning of the school year and again at the end to assess areas of growth and to identify needed areas of personal and behavioral change.

| Strategy | Level 1 | Level 2 | Level 3 | Level 4 | Level 5 | Score Circle One |
|---|---|---|---|---|---|---|
| **1. Invest in comprehensive professional development for all adults to support student learning.** | Investment in professional development is uneven and not comprehensive. The principal approves individual teacher requests for participation in professional development experiences beyond those planned for the entire faculty. | Investment in professional development is provided for the principal and teachers as required by local, state, national or federal programs. Professional development experiences are often contracted and occur as an event, part of opening the school year or as a scheduled release day. Although the experiences may be of high quality, they are rarely connected or embedded in teaching and learning practice. | The principal and some teacher leaders decide how to best invest in the instructional capacity of some teachers based on student performance data. Professional development experiences are usually focused on a particular instructional strategy, student skill or assessment technique within grades or possibly across grades. | The principal supports a systemic approach to investing in various types of professional development for all teachers and some staff and stakeholders that continuously builds adult capacity throughout the year. The school leadership uses student results to weed out professional development investments where there is no evidence of direct connection to student learning needs and performance. | The principal and teachers ensure that investment in all adult learning is directly tied to student learning and development needs. The principal ensures that all professional development models quality teaching practices and produces measurable changes in teaching and learning. The principal and teachers seek external resources for complementary professional development in order to maximize the effect of the investment. | 1 2 3 4 5 |
| **2. Align the schoolwide professional development plan with school and learning goals.** | A schoolwide comprehensive professional development plan does not exist. The principal approves a few teacher requests to attend conferences or other professional development opportunities, and does not participate in instructional leadership experiences. | Professional development, which may be aligned to explicit school or learning goals, is provided for the principal and teachers as specifically required by local, state, national or federal mandates. | The principal and teacher leaders jointly identify priority professional development for all teachers and some staff for the entire year. The principal, as an instructional leader, engages some teacher leaders in examining student performance data to align individual and collective professional development to their learning needs and those of their students. | The principal leads a schoolwide dialogue to shape a comprehensive professional development plan and individual teacher growth plans, both of which align with the core values and vision of the school. The principal supports ongoing professional development through formal and informal interactions about instruction, conducts learning walkthroughs and connects teachers to effective practices. | The principal ensures that a comprehensive professional development plan is aligned with standards in the field and school learning goals. The principal monitors the implementation of the plan for rigor and relevance for adult learning and to ensure experiences are focused, require application of new knowledge and skills, are based on student learning data and are analyzed to identify new gaps in adult or student learning. | 1 2 3 4 5 |

1 Learning Centered
2 Diverse Communities
3 21st Century Learners
4 Quality Instruction
5 Knowledge and Data
6 Community Engagement

| Strategy | Level 1 | Level 2 | Level 3 | Level 4 | Level 5 | Score Circle One |
|---|---|---|---|---|---|---|
| 3. Encourage adults to broaden networks to bring new knowledge and resources to learning environments. | The principal does not promote or expect regular networking or outreach activities to bring new knowledge and resources in to the school. There are no formal structures to share knowledge and resources within the school. | There is minimal sharing of knowledge and resources through formal networks. Most often the networks are connected to requirements of local, state, national or federal mandates. | The principal and many teachers regularly network informally and formally through learning communities and action research projects to share diverse resources and knowledge with the intent to transform teaching practices to meet individual student learning needs and increase performance. | The principal regularly encourages teachers and other adults to connect and share knowledge, skills and diverse resources by building relationships and networks through existing learning communities within the school, district and nation. The principal encourages teachers to learn how technology can effectively support networking and to access new instructional resources. | The principal, all teachers and some stakeholders create, lead, participate and sustain local, state, national and international networks as a key strategy for accessing new knowledge and diverse resources to increase student and adult performance. The principal models effective use of technology to support networking and accessing resources for instructional leadership development and benchmarking of effective operational practices. | 1 2 3 4 5 |
| 4. Provide time, structures and opportunities for adults to plan, work, reflect and celebrate together to improve practice. | There are little or no opportunities and no formal structures for joint planning or reflection. | There is some joint planning and reflection to satisfy requirements of local, state, national or federal mandates. | The principal supports teaching and learning by creating a flexible schedule that provides time and space for joint planning, work, reflection and celebration. The principal encourages teachers to participate in formal learning communities to examine disaggregated student performance data and agree on a few instructional strategies that better support individual and group learning needs. | The principal and all teachers participate in and support multiple ongoing internal professional learning communities that are led by teachers or instructional leaders. Learning communities reflect on current practice and examine formative and summative performance data to reach collective agreement on needed interventions and changes in instructional practices for adults. Student and adult achievements are regularly celebrated. | The principal sustains the learning culture by constantly managing collaborative structures to address the changing learning needs of students and adults. By including stakeholders and using technology, the principal encourages individual leadership to enhance planning, reflection and work of the school. Celebration of adult and student learning permeates the daily culture. | 1 2 3 4 5 |

# For More Information

## On the Web

**The National Staff Development Council** (www.nsdc.org) provides a range of online tools, including a library of staff development resources that help educators engage in professional learning.

**The Teacher Professional Development Sourcebook** (www.teachersourcebook.org) is a free online guide from Editorial Projects in Education on teacher professional development. Each issue includes resources, research and professional development events dedicated to helping teachers improve their practice.

## Resources and Research

Delehant, A. M. *Making Meetings Work: How to Get Started, Get Going, and Get It Done.* Thousand Oaks, CA: Corwin Press, 2007.

This book offers step-by-step planning processes designed for principals, teacher leaders, staff developers and trainers. The guide is packed with tools, strategies and tips for planning meetings and helping groups work effectively together.

Fogarty, R., and B. Pete. *From Staff Room to Classroom: A Guide for Planning and Coaching Professional Learning.* Thousand Oaks, CA: Corwin Press, 2006.

The book offers useful tips for working with teachers using mentoring and coaching scenarios. This guide presents techniques for customizing professional development and workshops, as well as how to put ideas into practice through the use of templates and practical suggestions.

Gordon, S. *Professional Development for School Improvement: Empowering Learning Communities.* Saddle River, NJ: Allyn & Bacon, 2004.

Eleven frameworks for school improvement that will help to build the capacity of individuals, teams and organizations to grow and develop are presented in this book. The author shows how professional development and school improvement need to have a focus on high quality teaching and learning.

Hord, S. M., and W. A. Sommers. *Leading Professional Learning Communities: Voices From Research and Practice.* Thousand Oaks, CA: Corwin Press, 2008.

The authors provide an accessible way to understand and learn from exemplary models of professional learning communities. The book covers building a vision for a professional learning community, implementing structures, creating policies and procedures, and developing the leadership skills required for initiating and sustaining a learning community.

# Manage data and knowledge to inform decisions and measure progress of student, adult and school performance.

1 Learning Centered

2 Diverse Communities

3 21st Century Learners

4 Quality Instruction

5 Knowledge and Data

6 Community Engagement

**T**he imperative to ensure high levels of learning for every child leaves little margin for error. Schools can no longer adopt programs and practices based on instincts; principals have to know that their schools' instructional and administrative practices will produce results.

Data can be a powerful tool for diagnosing and improving school programs and instruction. But, in many cases, the major challenge schools face is not finding the data but determining what is most relevant. In the past decade, the amount of data on student, school and teacher performance has multiplied. A wealth of data exists about school programs and performance. But not all of it is pertinent, or understandable. As they struggle to discern meaning from multiple data sources, effective school leaders continually ask this essential question: So what?

School leaders and teachers are increasing their use of formative data, balanced with summative data, to work with individual students on improving specific skills. Principals use multiple measures of summative data over time—showing the growth in learning of individual students allows the school to be more accountable

Unless you have the capacity to analyze data, you're data-rich, but information-poor.

Terrence Young

and to assess what it did, or didn't do, to encourage progress. Growth measures can help identify which concepts and skills are present or missing, which teachers teach those concepts and skills better than their peers, and whether the growth is developmentally moving along or surpassing predictable growth based on the expected development process.

In addition to the summative data that the NCLB Act or the state assessment system requires once a year, teachers want more data at more frequent intervals to monitor the progress of skill development in individual students. A strong body of research shows that regular, formative assessments improve student learning by giving students feedback on their progress and teachers information they can use in real time to modify their instruction. In some cases, such assessments can involve something as simple as asking the right questions to determine if students understand the lesson. Formative assessment includes the tests that individual teachers use as a point-in-time check on how students are doing.

Parents and the public are also calling for accountability for student learning from both teachers and administrators. Beyond examining trends based on data of student learning, emphasis on teacher quality and its relationship to student achievement has reinforced the need to assess instructional skills and instructional leadership as well. Gone are the days when seat time in mandated workshops constitutes effective professional development for adults in a learning community. Instead, the performance of adults is more and more tied to the performance of students.

## A CLOSER LOOK

### Inform, Inspire and Improve

Just for the Kids (JFTK), sponsored by the National Center for Educational Achievement, is a program that helps educators promote a vision that leads to all students succeeding. JFTK focuses on benchmarking and comparing against the best schools using three methods: inform, inspire and improve.

- **Inform with data.** Compare your performance with schools that have successfully overcome similar challenges.

- **Inspire with evidence-based practices.** Learn from the practices of high-performing schools.

- **Improve through focused actions.** Set academic goals and steps for implementing.

Source: National Center for Educational Achievement, Just for the Kids (www.just4kids.org).

The use of technology is making data more easily accessible than ever before. Districts and schools are creating digital portfolios that allow students, teachers and principals to see samples of student work online. These portfolios give additional information on student achievement to supplement test scores and provide a window into classroom instruction. In addition, student data systems can help teachers receive timely information to improve teaching practice. Data systems can also give educators, parents and policymakers the information they need to improve student learning.

Schools also are expected to show indicators that they are meeting the developmental needs of the child. Pre-kindergarten students, for example, are evaluated against readiness indicators. Out-of-school programs are evaluated for their quality and effectiveness in enriching student learning and well-being. And students are evaluated against health standards and other measures.

What does it look like when principals lead the management of data and knowledge to inform decision-making and measure progress? We see principals who:

- **Make performance data a primary driver for school improvement**

- **Measure student, adult and school performance using a variety of data**

- **Build capacity of adults and students to use knowledge effectively to make decisions**

- **Benchmark high-achieving schools with comparable demographics**

- **Make results transparent to the entire school community**

1 Learning Centered
2 Diverse Communities
3 21st Century Learners
4 Quality Instruction
5 Knowledge and Data
6 Community Engagement

## A CLOSER LOOK

### Using Data to Drive Improvement

Schools across the nation are using data more than ever to make decisions. In fact, the amount of data available to principals and teachers can sometimes be overwhelming. Schools are using longitudinal and formative assessments to provide an accurate representation of student achievement. Longitudinal assessments, providing a "big picture" look at achievement, allow schools to follow a student's progress over time. Formative assessments, providing a snapshot of achievement, allow teachers to target instruction and interventions. There are a number of ways schools can use longitudinal data to improve student performance, such as:

- **External benchmarking.** Comparing the performance of your school with other schools outside of your district to determine if your school is performing to its full potential and to look for best practices.

- **Internal benchmarking.** Comparing the performance of your school with other schools within your district to look for best practices.

- **Validation of performance standards.** Examining student results over time to gauge whether high performance continues in later grades.

- **Program evaluation.** Following participants and nonparticipants over time to determine program effectiveness.

- **Understanding relationships and trends.** Tracking students over time, paying close attention to changes and the factors that might be responsible for the changes.

- **Diagnosis and prescription.** Analyzing data on individual students over the course of years to identify problem areas and to make adjustments in instruction or services.

School leaders should focus on analyzing data and comparing results with others schools to identify strengths and weaknesses. Improvement plans should be based on the analysis, and resources allocated accordingly. Leaders must also ensure that teachers have opportunities to use data individually and in teams to gauge the effectiveness of their instruction. Finally, leaders should provide continuous professional development for principals and teachers on how to use data as a tool.

Source: Laird, E. *Data Use Drives School and District Improvement.* Council of Chief State School Officers and Data Quality Campaign, 2006.

## Make performance data a primary driver for school improvement

Improvement begins only when people are willing to make honest and diligent efforts to create a deep understanding of current performance. Effective leaders are skilled at focusing on the most important data and bringing it to the forefront so it can be analyzed to inform changes that make sense for the school's staff and community. They look for patterns that suggest an effective program that needs to be maintained or expanded or a challenge that needs to be addressed.

The use of data and research is particularly important to inform teaching and learning practices. For example, overall data might show that a school is doing well in mathematics, but a closer analysis might reveal an achievement gap between girls and boys. Leaders can then engage teachers and others in analyzing this data more closely to determine possible causes that might suggest possible solutions. Vertical and horizontal learning communities can look at data to understand the connections between and within grade levels and content areas.

If we only knew what we know, we would be astonished at the treasures contained in our knowledge.

Immanuel Kant

To provide the most effective instruction for every student, teachers must apply approaches that produce results. To do so, they need regular, high-quality data that will enable them to gauge the impact of their instruction and make adjustments when necessary. This requires regular access—daily, weekly, monthly, quarterly—to formative data, which indicates progress on knowledge and skill development, that supplements and provides more ready information than traditional summative data, such as annual state assessments, which often are not available in a timely manner.

Schools must develop students who meet state benchmarks and who are prepared for academic or career success. Tracking progress toward college and career readiness provides essential information needed to assess the progress of all students, regardless of current skill levels. Effective leaders work collaboratively with the school community to analyze student qualitative and quantitative data to get an accurate picture of growth and development of the whole child and to develop strategies to respond to the implications of the data. Effective leaders meet regularly with the school staff and partners to examine data on teacher and school performance and its implications for community support.

1 Learning Centered
2 Diverse Communities
3 21st Century Learners
4 Quality Instruction
5 Knowledge and Data
6 Community Engagement

## Measure student, adult and school performance using a variety of data

Effective school leaders don't try to hide the results of performance assessments of students, adults and the entire school; they use data to analyze progress toward meeting shared performance goals. School leaders face demands for timely, accurate and individualized data. Teachers need timely data on students entering their classrooms, particularly when those students are recent transfers from other districts. Educators, parents and policymakers need to identify early academic goals that prepare students for success in education, work and life. Educators and community members increasingly want to find out whether individual students are on track to be prepared for success after high school. Educators need to identify consistently high-performing schools as benchmarks to pinpoint and study best practices.

Effective learning communities collect, analyze and discuss multiple sources of data to assess:

• **Student performance.** When looking at individual student performance, leaders collect, analyze and share numerous sources of data. Some states track individual student test scores, as well as enrollment, attendance, behavior and graduation data. Learning communities look periodically at formative data, such as assessments developed by individual classroom teachers as well as mandated standardized tests. In addition, instructional leaders can collect elementary and middle school test score data and match these records over time using a statewide student identifier. This helps members of the learning community predict how to build on success or what interventions to use. By collecting student data on completion of advanced courses in middle school, for instance, school leaders get a better idea of whether students who leave the eighth grade are capable of taking advanced courses in high school and becoming well prepared for success in college and beyond. In addition to assessing academic performance, schools and community organizations are working to develop a broad range of social, emotional and physical outcomes that measure the development of the whole child.

Students play important roles in monitoring their own learning. Cognitive research suggests that children learn best when they can assess themselves and make their own improvements. Such assessments indicate that students have internalized the standards they are expected to meet and can evaluate what they know and are able to do.

- **Teacher performance.** Emphasis on teacher quality and its relationship to student achievement has made teacher evaluation an area of increased concern for school leaders. Several districts and states are working on the design of a fair performance-based teacher evaluation system tied to student performance results. And a number of progressive school leaders are treating teacher evaluation as an organizational responsibility that includes improving school climate. Principals who serve as instructional leaders assess teacher performance by linking teacher evaluation to professional development, school goals and student learning. Many school leaders are also looking at ways to meaningfully involve teachers in their own evaluation and peer review.

- **Principal performance.** Effective leaders of learning communities hold themselves and others responsible for realizing high standards of performance for students' academic and social learning. Yet, leadership assessment and feedback remains an important missing link to improving and strengthening school leadership. When it comes to assessing principals, most school leadership programs focus on mandated professional development hours, mentoring, licensing policies and standards—while, according to findings from research at Vanderbilt University, minimal attention is paid to job-embedded continuous assessment, feedback and subsequent action. Through a combination of formal and informal self-assessments, leaders of learning communities should be evaluated on leadership behaviors associated with student learning and management practice results.

- **School performance.** Collecting performance data on the entire school becomes increasingly important in climates of choice and accountability. Pinpointing the strengths and weaknesses of school programs in addressing student learning needs is not only an essential part of a continuous improvement process but also helps demonstrate yearly progress goals, a key factor in parent choice of schools for their children.

A growing number of school districts are using computer "dashboards" or "scorecards" to show how students are doing school by school. In Boston, teachers can tap into a dashboard on their laptops to see the academic history of each of their students. The system also provides school- and district-level information, so that principals can look at achievement across classrooms, and district officials can look at how various schools are performing. Dashboards are an integral tool to achieving real alignment—getting all constituents focused on the right issues and the right measures of success. Dashboards are also important communication tools, indicating to everyone which data should be watched in moving the school community toward its goals.

Effective leaders give students, teachers and parents access to academic performance and developmental growth data. They share the results on school performance with researchers and community organizations so that everyone can help improve student, adult and school performance.

1 Learning Centered
2 Diverse Communities
3 21st Century Learners
4 Quality Instruction
5 Knowledge and Data
6 Community Engagement

## INSIDE A SCHOOL: A FOCUS ON PRACTICE

**Naples Elementary School, Naples, Italy**
**Principal Richard R. Alix**

Richard R. Alix created a culture of data-driven school improvement from the moment he arrived at Naples Elementary School in 2004. Under the Department of Defense schools' mandatory rotation policy for principals, Alix replaced a principal who had been transferred to another school. The first thing he did was examine the data on student achievement and he saw that test scores had declined over the previous five years.

To create a sense of urgency among the school staff to improve results, he prepared a slide show at the second faculty meeting of the year. "An eerie silence engulfed the room as teachers began to reflect on the data," Alix says. But, he notes, "the questions that were framed reflected a high degree of professionalism from most members of the professional staff. This was encouraging and motivating."

In response, he asked the school's literacy team to come up with a solution, and the team proposed additional reading assessments and support for preparing teachers to use the assessment effectively. The team also met monthly to review data, identify progress and brainstorm solutions to obstacles. At the end of the first year, more than 80 percent of the third grade students were at or above grade level, compared with 40 percent when Alix began at Naples. And results have continued to improve since then.

The school also publishes its achievement data widely and created a data display in the central office to show to prospective military families. To Alix, the emphasis on data has enabled everyone in the school to put their attention on what matters. "The focus on quantitative data continues to empower teachers, parents and students to make effective decisions," he says.

**1** Learning Centered

**2** Diverse Communities

**3** 21st Century Learners

**4** Quality Instruction

**5** Knowledge and Data

**6** Community Engagement

## Build capacity of adults and students to use knowledge effectively to make decisions

Management consultant Peter Drucker once said there was no such thing as "knowledge management." Instead, he said, it is all about managing knowledgeable people. Knowledge is useful information, aligned to beliefs, commitment and action, directed at achieving a particular result. Knowledge is also about meaning, requiring that information is both context-specific and relational. Each of these defining characteristics of knowledge indicates the important role of the people who create, process, interpret and transfer it to create knowledgeable people.

The ability to lead and manage knowledgeable people increases in importance as the speed and scope of information-sharing increases. Information technologies—such as information resources management, knowledge databases and collaborative tools—act as catalysts that enable and facilitate the process of knowledge sharing. Effective school leaders know they have to create appropriate learning environments in which to share meaningful information. They also must build the capacity of everyone in their schools to use information wisely as a tool to achieve their school vision.

Leaders of learning communities always seek to enhance the flow of tacit knowledge by establishing a sharing culture, facilitating human interaction and socialization, and intelligently managing human resources. They are avid and savvy consumers of research and ensure that teachers and staff members stay on top of the latest knowledge about effective programs and practices. They—and their leadership teams—are adept at sifting through data to determine what decisions and actions will better support student and adult learning. They communicate the analyses to community stakeholders so they will understand the implications for school and community instructional programs.

Effective principals work with their staff members to conduct regular, multiple formative assessments of student learning, meet regularly to make meaning of the data and use the results to drive learning. They work with other organizations and agencies to collect and analyze data outside the school. Together, the school leader and the school's partners gather information on a broad set of outcomes to ensure that the school and its partners are developing children's full set of abilities.

Partnerships with different sectors of the community help build the capacity of schools to analyze and use data effectively. By providing statistical and data analysis expertise, these partners help principals collect and interpret a much broader array of information on schools. Collective knowledge illuminates and informs shared decisions.

Within a climate of continuous improvement, the question driving the leadership curiosity of the principal is: How can the school find out what it does not know?

## Benchmark high-achieving schools with comparable demographics

In a climate of mounting pressure to demonstrate higher levels of proficiency on higher standards than ever before, a considerable gap in effective practice still exists. With the new emphasis on learning goals (academic standards or performance targets) and outcomes (usually on state-level, criterion-referenced tests), school and district leaders are left to determine the best way to address this gap.

Furthermore, finite time and human and financial resources require that educators become selective and deliberate in the improvement initiatives they undertake. Identifying best practices and benchmarking their schools against other high-performing schools of comparable demographics helps focus educators on the practices and strategies that are likely to have deep and positive impacts on student and adult learning.

Effective leaders find evidence from the best schools schools that are similar to their own in terms of numbers of students, low-income students, English language learners, and racial and ethnic breakdowns. By comparing their school's performance with that of schools that have effectively overcome similar challenges, and comparing their practices with those of higher-performing schools, effective leaders can inform and inspire better practice. But moving an organization from *knowing* what high-performing schools do to *doing* what those schools do requires focused planning. In effective learning communities, knowledge gained from school comparisons can then be used to guide deliberate action.

## INSIDE A SCHOOL: A FOCUS ON PRACTICE

**Taylor Ray Elementary School, Rosenberg, Texas**
**Principal Diane Parks**

Students at Taylor Ray Elementary take a lot of tests—state tests in four subjects at every grade, district tests, and school-based reading assessments and computer-based tests. But that's just fine for Principal Diane Parks and her team because the test results give them a wealth of data to use to monitor student progress and determine appropriate instructional strategies.

The school's core team, which includes Parks, the assistant principal, instructional specialists, the counselor and special education teachers, look at the results broken down by student demographic groups and objectives. They go over the data by grade level to see how students are performing and, most important, what the results suggest they need to do next to improve performance.

"We talk about where we are, where we need to be, and ask, 'So what?'" Parks says. "Now that we've got the information, what do we do with it? That's the important part of the data meeting. What are the interventions kids are going to get?"

In addition to the core team, Taylor Ray has also formed "vertical" teams that cross grade levels and focus on the core academic subjects. Like the core team, the vertical teams examine data on student performance and look at evidence from classrooms to help share successful practices. For example, if a third grade classroom has shown success in reading, other teachers can benefit from understanding that classroom's strategies.

To Parks, the practices work because the entire staff is committed to improving outcomes for all students, and to doing whatever it takes to produce those outcomes. "It's from the trust we've built," Parks says. "When we have data meetings, we're talking about kids."

1 Learning Centered

2 Diverse Communities

3 21st Century Learners

4 Quality Instruction

5 Knowledge and Data

6 Community Engagement

**TERMS TO KNOW**

### Action Research

Action research is a process that involves reflection, inquiry, planning, action and assessment of the results of the action. Teams identify questions or problems, design strategies, collect, analyze and share data, and discuss the findings to improve administrative or teaching and learning practices.

As part of the process, students, teachers, researchers, principals, other staff and community members examine the school environment: how the school operates, how teachers teach and how well students learn.

The key component of action research is that it is a recurring, cyclical process that focuses on improvement. Many community organizations and businesses involved in quality processes refer to action research as the Deming Cycle, a four-step problem-solving and change process: Plan, Do, Check, Act (PDCA).

Below is an example of an action research project by Goldys, Kruft and Subrizi from their article, "Action Research: Do It Yourself!"

**Objective:** Using real-life experiences to increase learning of difficult math skills.

**Research:** Difficult math skills for students were identified by summative testing. Activities were then designed to allow targeted students to apply skills to real-life experiences. The students were then retested on the skills.

| Sample Units | Skill | Real-Life Experience |
|---|---|---|
| Addition and subtraction | Choosing operations for story problems | |
| Place value | Finding greater numbers | |
| Money | Adding with regrouping | |
| Subtraction | Getting information from a table | |
| Multiplication | Increasing batches | |
| Division | Explaining division | |

**Results:** Retest scores were higher after real-life experiences for 85 percent of students and were the same for 15 percent of students. No student scored lower on any retest item after participating in real-life experiences.

Sources: Goldys, P., C. Kruft and P. Subrizi. "Action Research: Do It Yourself." *Principal*, Vol. 86, No. 4. Alexandria, VA: National Association of Elementary School Principals, 2007.

LeTendre, B. G. "Six Steps to a Solution." *Journal of Staff Development*, Vol. 21, No. 3. Oxford, OH: National Staff Development Council, 2000.

Mills, G. Action Research: *A Guide for the Teacher Researcher*. Upper Saddle River, NJ: Merrill Prentice Hall, 2003.

Sagor, R. *The Action Research Guidebook*. Thousand Oaks, CA: Corwin Press, 2005.

Having objectively evaluated its current reality—including student performance data and instructional practices—a school will set student academic goals and articulate the practices to be used in reaching those goals. In highly effective learning communities, planning will lead to changes in the behavior of adults and subsequently in the performance levels of students.

In addition to comparing teaching and instructional practices, effective school leaders know that they must also benchmark their administrative and operations practices in order to channel as many resources as possible into instruction. And, as the economy gets tighter, administrators can expect more money to be taken out of operations. Effective leaders compare their operational practices, including billing, invoicing, accounts payable, transportation, and heating, fuel and energy costs against well-established benchmarks within the community and nationally. They use benchmarks that are developed by school systems as well as those used by other local or relevant systems in business or government. Whichever points of comparison they use, school leaders know that running a lean and effective operation is more important than ever.

## Make results transparent to the entire school community

School leaders present complex data in ways that are fair and actionable. They know this is the first step toward more effective schools and higher-achieving students. Over the past decade, schools have increasingly produced voluminous reports on their progress and made them available to the school community, often over the Internet. Under the NCLB Act, this process has accelerated. Now schools are required to produce annual report cards showing a wealth of data on their performance.

These reports, while informative, have not always been as useful as they could be. Parents say that the data is not always comprehensible, and they can't always tell what sense they should make of the information for their child. Teachers, as well, often have difficulty "making meaning" of the data for their work.

## A CLOSER LOOK

### Notifying Parents of School Improvement Status

Principals are stepping up contact with parents about a wide range of data-related information. Knowing what to say, how to say it and when to say it can be a challenge. Here are a few tips for communicating with parents about your school's improvement status:

- **Provide key information.** Make notices brief. Fairly and accurately explain the reasons that the school was designated for improvement and describe your plan of action for improvement. Inform parents of their rights and opportunities that are available as a result of the designation, such as school choice or supplemental educational services (SES).

- **Hold meetings for discussion.** Schedule one or more meetings to discuss the designation and what it means for the school, the community and parents.

- **Make sure parents understand options before having to decide.** Give parents time to consider their options before making any decisions about transferring their child to another school or participating in SES programs. Also, make sure parents have all of the necessary information about potential transfer schools and SES providers and programs, including transportation.

Examples of notices for notifying parents of school improvement status, as well as samples for notifying parents of report cards and SES opportunities, are available in *It Takes a Parent: Transforming Education in the Wake of the No Child Left Behind Act*, online at: www.appleseednetwork.org/Portals/0/Documents/Publications/TransfomEduNoChildLeft.pdf.

Source: Coleman, A., A. Starzynski, S. Winnick, S. Palmer and J. Furr. *It Takes a Parent: Transforming Education in the Wake of the No Child Left Behind Act.* Washington, D.C. : Appleseed, 2006.

Effective leaders are skillful at finding useful data—and making sure it is used. They work with school communities to determine what the data means and how it might affect their programs. Leaders communicate the data widely so that all stakeholders are aware of what the findings show and what they suggest about the school. Such communication helps build support for the school by providing stakeholders with information about the school's successes and challenges with student and adult learning. It also empowers individuals throughout the school community to suggest possible solutions.

In Mobile County, Alabama, for example, the school system and the Mobile Area Education Foundation are using a high level of transparency and communication about data throughout the community to build support for changes in policy, personnel and practice. All 100 schools in the Mobile County school system have developed a data-driven dashboard to focus on raising the bar and closing the achievement gap. In addition, school-system-generated quarterly criterion-referenced tests provide data on student progress in meeting grade-level benchmarks in core academic areas. All principals have been trained to lead and monitor implementation of research-based best strategies matched to individual school needs. Supplemental services are aligned to address individual student learning needs in all schools.

To collect and report on a broad set of indicators of youth development, principals work with community agencies and organizations to develop measures of children's growth and development. In some cases, the leaders might find that the data does not exist. In that case, they work with community agencies and partners to develop it. Collectively, the school and organizations report to the community. The combined report provides a picture of young people's knowledge, health and well-being that no single agency or school can provide.

1 Learning Centered

2 Diverse Communities

3 21st Century Learners

4 Quality Instruction

5 Knowledge and Data

6 Community Engagement

# ? | Standard 5: Reflection Questions

1. How can administrators, teachers, parents, students and community members analyze data more effectively to improve student, adult and school performance?

2. How are schools with comparable demographics that demonstrate high performance for all students increasing student learning?

3. Is the reflection tool that asks, "Why?," at least five times being used to make meaning of data by "drilling deeper" to support learning needs more effectively?

4. How adaptive is the teaching and learning environment to changing practices based on continuous examination of formative performance data to better support learning needs?

5. How can timely access to current research and knowledge about effective teaching, learning and child development become part of continuous learning and improve practice?

6. What learning communities can best deepen the dialogue about investments in teaching and learning and youth development based on research and experience?

7. How can the relevancy and transparency of data for all stakeholders be improved?

8. How can evaluation systems for teachers and administrators better support continuous learning and increase performance for students and adults?

# Standard 5: Action Steps

After answering the Reflection Questions, list the action steps needed to attain the learning goals specific to each question:

| Reflection Question | Action Step(s) | Who needs to take the lead? Who needs to be involved? |
|---|---|---|
| 1 | | |
| 2 | | |
| 3 | | |
| 4 | | |
| 5 | | |
| 6 | | |
| 7 | | |
| 8 | | |

1 Learning Centered
2 Diverse Communities
3 21st Century Learners
4 Quality Instruction
5 Knowledge and Data
6 Community Engagement

## Standard 5: Leadership Continuum

This self-assessment continuum is intended to help you move toward higher levels of leadership. Consider using this tool at the beginning of the school year and again at the end to assess areas of growth and to identify needed areas of personal and behavioral change.

| Strategy | Level 1 | Level 2 | Level 3 | Level 4 | Level 5 | Score Circle One |
|---|---|---|---|---|---|---|
| **1. Make performance data a primary driver for school improvement.** | School performance data exists, but is not easily accessible or deeply analyzed by the principal, teachers or stakeholders. | The principal maintains achievement, financial, facilities, transportation and human resource data needed to comply with local, state, national and federal mandates. | The principal and few key leaders advance a culture of measurement and data-based decision-making, but there is limited schoolwide communication about implications of the data for changing administrative or instructional practices. | The principal ensures all teachers and staff have timely access to quality student and administrative operations data, and the principal and teachers regularly analyze performance trends and effectiveness of practices. Data analysis is shared with the school community to promote understanding of changes in practice. | The principal, teachers and stakeholders expect full access to all data that measures the quality of student performance and management of operations of the school learning community. Intentional conversations regularly explore the link between the implications of performance data and improved practice. | 1 2 3 4 5 |
| **2. Measure student, adult and school performance using a variety of data.** | Measurement of performance adheres to district policy and schedules. | In addition to performance measurements required by law, some measures of student learning or development may be required because of partnership initiatives. | The principal explores with some community agencies, organizations and businesses new measures of youth growth and development, academic learning and adult performance in order to obtain a clearer picture of school performance. | The principal, teacher leaders and some community leaders coordinate the joint implementation of expanded data collection, analysis and reporting to the school community on the condition of youth growth and development, student and adult learning, and advancement toward the school's vision. | The principal engages teachers, stakeholders and district staff in creating new or modifying existing performance evaluation and accountability systems for student and adult learning. The systems include a variety of data: formative and summative, disaggregated and trend, quantitative and qualitative, and self-assessment and external assessment. | 1 2 3 4 5 |

| Strategy | Level 1 | Level 2 | Level 3 | Level 4 | Level 5 | Score Circle One |
|----------|---------|---------|---------|---------|---------|------------------|
| **3. Build capacity of adults and students to use knowledge effectively to make decisions.** | Limited data is available to all stakeholders and is seldom used to inform program, instructional or administrative operational decisions. | The principal maintains a variety of data required by local, state, national or federal mandates that is seldom shared with the school community in making decisions. | The principal engages teachers in learning how to use data to inform schoolwide dialogue and reinforce a data-based decision-making culture. | The principal, many teachers, some students and community partners analyze data regularly to monitor the effectiveness of their work and make decisions about changes to improve learning. | The principal, teachers, staff, students and stakeholders are regularly engaged in data gathering and analysis and view data as fundamental in guiding decisions and creating systemic interventions to improve student, adult and school performance. | 1 2 3 4 5 |
| **4. Benchmark high-achieving schools with comparable demographics.** | Comparing school performance with other schools, except those in the immediate geographical vicinity, is not an explicit or recurring practice. | Comparing school performance with other schools most often occurs only when required by local, state, national or federal mandates. | The principal and teacher leaders periodically research and examine the performance of a few schools locally or within the state that have shown achievement gains or effective practices. | The principal and most teachers regularly research and examine benchmark practices and performance of high-achieving schools with comparable demographics within the state or nation. | The principal, teachers and many community leaders systematically search for benchmarks of administrative operations and instructional practices used by high-performing schools to meet specific student or adult learning needs. | 1 2 3 4 5 |
| **5. Make results transparent to the entire school community.** | School results are formally released when requested, and often provided in non-user-friendly language and formats. The school and community rarely interact about data. There is no system to build community understanding of the implications of the data. | The school community is notified of results as required by local, state, national or federal mandates or external funders. The principal may ask the community to provide responses to the data as input for possible ways to improve performance. | The principal and lead teachers provide performance results to students, parents and interested community organizations in an understandable format and open and timely manner. Some parents and community members participate on a regular basis in developing strategies for some students with specific learning needs. | The principal, most teachers, some students and community leaders regularly examine results to develop strategies to improve student, adult and school performance. There is a strong effort made to present data to the school community in a more user-friendly format to create substantive dialogue and action to improve student and adult performance. | The principal, teachers and many students, parents and community leaders seek to make the entire community aware of school results data. Every effort is made to ensure that the data and resulting knowledge is understood by all stakeholders and guides joint discussion and action about high-yield school and community strategies to increase student and adult performance. | 1 2 3 4 5 |

1 Learning Centered

2 Diverse Communities

3 21st Century Learners

4 Quality Instruction

5 Knowledge and Data

6 Community Engagement

# For More Information

## On the Web

**Arkansas Leadership Academy** (www.arkleadership.org) and **Illinois Principals Association** (www. ilprincipals.org) provide Principal Leadership Performance Rubrics on their Web sites. These self-assessments measure a principal's leadership skills with a focus on improving the following five areas: Creating and Living the Mission, Vision and Beliefs; Leading and Managing Change; Developing Deep Knowledge about Teaching and Learning; Building and Maintaining Collaborative Relationships; and Building and Sustaining Accountability Systems.

**Brevard County Public School District** in Florida is recognized as a high-performing, data-based decision-making district by the Florida Sterling Council. Its Web-based "Score card" (www.brevard.k12.fl.us/ScoreCard/main.html) measures school performance based on Brevard Public Schools' Strategic Plan and each school's improvement plan and can be used for best practices.

**The Education Trust** (www.edtrust.org) provides resources to use in schools, communities and states to call attention to achievement gaps, find schools that are closing the gaps and learn about practices that enable all students to achieve at high levels. The Web site includes an interactive database that can help benchmark and compare best practices in different schools.

**Mid-continent Research for Education and Learning** has a dedicated section, Assessment/Accountability/Data Use (www.mcrel.org/topics/Assessment/), on its Web site about effectively using data. The section is rich with resources, best practices, and workshop and training models.

**SchoolNet** (www.schoolnet.com) provides a Web-based, user-friendly dashboard product for making data relevant, accessible and actionable. The Web site also has free resources on data and assessment as well as case studies and videos on best practices.

## Resources and Research

Boudett, K. P., E. City and R. Murnane, eds. *Data Wise: A Step-by-Step Guide to Using Assessment Results to Improve Teaching and Learning.* **Cambridge, MA: Harvard Education Publishing Group, 2005.**

This book shows how examining classroom data can become a catalyst for important school community conversations. These conversations will help to identify obstacles to change, foster collaboration and enhance the school culture and climate.

Caro-Bruce, C., R. Flessner, M. Klehr and K. Zeichner. *Creating Equitable Classrooms Through Action Research.* **Thousand Oaks, CA: Corwin Press, 2007.**

This book uses action research to address inequity in public education. Included are case studies, examples and guidelines for developing an action research project.

Danielson, C., and T. McGreal. *Teacher Evaluation to Enhance Professional Practice.* **Alexandria, VA: Association for Supervision and Curriculum Development (ASCD), 2000.**

With concrete examples and assessment tools, this book discusses effective teacher evaluation systems that combine quality assurance with professional development for all teachers. Charlotte Danielson's framework for professional practice is currently part of many teacher evaluation systems.

# Actively engage the community to create shared responsibility for student performance and development.

1 Learning Centered
2 Diverse Communities
3 21st Century Learners
4 Quality Instruction
5 Knowledge and Data
6 Community Engagement

**E**ducators, policymakers and families increasingly agree: Schools simply cannot do it alone. Children need numerous opportunities to learn and develop—at home, in school and in the community.

As Vince Ferrandino, chair of the task force that created the publication *A New Day for Learning*, wrote, "No one believes that children stop learning when the bell rings at the end of the school day. Curiosity bubbles inside the minds of children from the moment they wake in the morning to when they go to bed at night. The challenge of learning communities is to encourage, connect and foster learning throughout a child's life—in school and beyond. How do we help children make sense of all the information and experiences in their lives? How do we ensure that all children have opportunities to reach their full potential in a competitive world where thinking skills are the most important asset of a society?"

The acknowledgement of the important role that parents and communities play in student achievement is unprecedented. In large urban districts, as well as smaller and rural ones, educators and public officials are focusing attention on community engagement as never before.

Active parent involvement is absolutely critical to raising student achievement.

Michael Bloomberg

In New York City, Mayor Michael Bloomberg has made parent involvement the third leg of his stool for improving public education in the city. Schools Chancellor Joel Klein assigned the responsibility for parent involvement to his deputy chancellor for teaching and learning. The idea in many communities is to go beyond the traditional role of parents supporting academic, social and athletic events, and to engage parents in ways that directly support student learning and development.

According to Collaborative Communications Group, which works deeply in parent and community engagement, the expansion of the parent role is occurring at three levels:

• **At the home and personal level**, where parents' understanding of parenting skills and ways to support their children's learning can be a support and extension of the learning day.

• **At the school level**, where parents need to understand school achievement data so they can compel and assist educators in making improvements based on that data.

• **At the public/community level**, where parents' understanding of test scores and data is required for informed public dialogue, community resource allocation and decision-making.

## A CLOSER LOOK

### Building Successful School, Family and Community Partnerships

Here are 10 steps for creating effective relationships from *School, Family, and Community Partnerships: Your Handbook for Action*:

- **Create an action team for partnerships**
- **Obtain funding and official support**
- **Provide training to all members of the action team for partnerships**
- **Identify starting points—present strengths and weaknesses**
- **Develop a three-year outline and vision for partnerships**
- **Write a one-year action plan**
- **Enlist staff, parents, students and the community to help conduct activities**
- **Evaluate implementations and results**
- **Conduct annual celebrations and report progress to all participants**
- **Continue to work toward a comprehensive, ongoing, goal-oriented program of partnerships**

Source: Epstein, J., M. Sanders, B. Simon, K. Clark Salinas, N. Rodriguez Jansorn and F. Van Voorhis. *School, Family, and Community Partnerships: Your Handbook for Action*. Second Edition. Thousand Oaks, CA: Corwin Press, 2002.

But involving parents isn't enough. In his article in *The New York Times Magazine*, "What No School Can Do," journalist James Traub predicts that even massive school improvement efforts will not be enough to reverse low achievement because reforming classrooms and schools is only part of the solution. Traub asserts that the conditions of students' lives *outside* the school have as much or more impact on students' school performance and social development than what goes on *inside* schools. If this is true, then it follows that parents need to be clear that their primary activity for childhood and adolescence should be to help children grow into healthy, well-developed individuals who can achieve in school.

Experience in many communities fortifies the notion that ignoring the community limits the potential impact of school improvement efforts. Furthermore, continuing to push community members aside is likely to have a negative effect: They may become opponents of improvement strategies rather than active participants in supporting them. Because parents and families are such key advocates for children, and because of the time children spend outside of school, failure to equip parents and others in the community with the skills, knowledge and expertise to be partners in the education process severely hampers progress toward learning.

What does it look like when principals lead through active community engagement? We see principals who:

- **Engage parents, families and the community to build relationships that support improved performance**

- **Serve as civic leaders who regularly engage with numerous stakeholders to support students, families and schools in more effective ways**

- **Shape partnerships to ensure multiple learning opportunities for students, in and out of school**

- **Market the school's distinctive learning environment and results to inform parents' choices of options that best fit their children's needs**

- **Advocate for high-quality education for every student**

1 Learning Centered
2 Diverse Communities
3 21st Century Learners
4 Quality Instruction
5 Knowledge and Data
6 Community Engagement

## A CLOSER LOOK

### Family Welcome Questionnaire

The link between family engagement and student achievement is strong. Parents who are more actively engaged in their child's education contribute to higher grades, increased test scores, higher graduation rates and higher enrollment in post-secondary education. To help educators forge strong relationships with parents, the authors of *Beyond the Bake Sale: The Essential Guide to Family-School Partnerships* have developed a set of questions to ask parents to help learn about students' families. It is recommended that parents be asked these questions face-to-face.

### Cultural background

• What languages are spoken in your home?

• In what country (or state) were you born?

• Tell us about your family's beliefs about the importance of education.

• What are your family traditions? What activities do you do as a family? How do you celebrate birthdays and other important family events?

• Who is in your extended family?

### Involvement at school and at home

• What are some ways you would like to be involved?

• What could the school do to help you be more involved?

• What are your working hours?

• When are the most convenient times for activities and meetings at school?

• What are your transportation needs?

• What are your hobbies, skills, talents and interests?

### Concerns, perspectives and ideas

• What would you like us to know about your child? What are his/her interests?

• What is working well for your child at school? What isn't?

• What are some ways you would like the school to recognize and teach about your child's culture?

• Are there any ways that you feel your culture could be better respected at school?

• Do you have some things that reflect your culture and background that you could share with us?

• How could you help the school reach out to other families in your community?

Source: Henderson, A., K. Mapp, V. Johnson and D. Davies. *Beyond the Bake Sale: The Essential Guide to Family-School Partnerships.* New York: New Press, 2007.

## Engage parents, families and the community to build relationships that support improved performance

Thirty years of research and a long history of state and federal legislation demonstrate what principals inherently know: The importance of parents as partners in schools cannot be overstated. The NCLB Act offered the first federal definition of parent involvement, which included the concept of "regular, two-way communication about student learning and other school activities."

Most parents and families, regardless of income, say they want their children to do well in school. Enough is known about the basics of good parenting and what parents can do to support student achievement to enable the design and organization of an ongoing system of opportunities for parents to learn how to help their children. The design and organization should be informed by data collected from parents and teachers in order to determine specific needs and interests and ensure that class offerings are appropriate.

Effective leaders take steps to ensure that all parents, regardless of home language or background, can be involved in the school in meaningful ways. School leaders reach out directly or enlist parent liaisons to reach out to parents and show them how to support their children's learning. They provide learning opportunities for parents. They provide materials in different languages and enlist staff members or parents who speak other languages to talk with non-English speaking parents. They and the teachers go to parents' homes, churches or community meetings to seek out parents reluctant to come into schools. The goal is to build a relationship of mutual accountability with each student's parents or family: Schools acknowledge the important link between parent involvement and student success, and parents acknowledge their responsibility for their children's learning.

Principals also keep teachers informed so that they can communicate to parents as well. Teachers are often the first line of contact with parents, and parents trust teachers' points of view. Principals foster school cultures that stress openness and communication. They make

**1** Learning Centered
**2** Diverse Communities
**3** 21st Century Learners
**4** Quality Instruction
**5** Knowledge and Data
**6** Community Engagement

## A CLOSER LOOK

### Scanning the Community

Continuous scanning of changes within different sectors of the community can help educators identify ways to engage the resources of the entire community to support student learning.

Research indicates all communities assign responsibility to eight sectors to sustain values that better everyone's lives through institutions, agencies and organizations. Educators can use the eight sectors as a systematic way to:

- **Gather all types of community voices—ideas, satisfaction feedback**
- **Identify varied partnerships including out-of-school learning opportunities**
- **Assess the spread of school strategic plan strategies to engage the community**
- **Identify multiple resources to support the needs of families and students**

The eight sectors are:

1. **Power**—Government, courts, unions

2. **Enlightenment**—Post-secondary education, research

3. **Wealth/poverty sector**—Property owners, business and industry, foundations, poverty programs, low-income population

4. **Well-being**—Health organizations, security and safety agencies

5. **Skill**—Public, proprietary, private and parochial schools, specialized training centers

6. **Affection**—Families and support groups

7. **Respect**—Civic organizations, service and volunteer organizations, honor societies, fraternities and sororities

8. **Rectitude**—Religious institutions, legal institutions

Source: Frazier, G. *Scan of the Community: Eight Sectors Tool.* International Center on Collaboration, adapted from Cunningham, Luvern L., *Educational Administration Quarterly*, Vol. 17, No. 2 (Spring, 1981) 21-43.

sure that teachers and other staff members communicate regularly with parents and other community members. In addition, they make sure that their schools present welcoming environments, and that everyone answers the phones and greets visitors warmly.

To be effective, leaders must be honest about schools. Public encounters can be awkward if the data on student learning progress isn't promising. But community members are more likely to support a school if the principal acknowledges the school's challenges, has an initial vision for needed changes and engages others in making meaning of the data and identifying new actions to support student learning in and out of school.

We haven't been a customer-sensitive kind of business. I think those days are over.

Joseph Murphy

### Serve as civic leaders who regularly engage with numerous stakeholders to support students, families and schools in more effective ways

Everyone has heard of the strategy of taking local civic leaders out of their roles and putting them into the principal's office to act as "Principal for a Day." But effective leaders of school learning communities know that their jobs require the reverse: They need to get out of the office and into the community. Effective principals are more than school leaders; they are civic leaders. Principals who serve as civic leaders make connections and build relationships in the surrounding neighborhood and the entire community. They meet regularly with elected officials, leaders of community or regional organizations, and parent groups to gauge their expectations for schools and explain how the school can meet those expectations. They search for ways community resources might better support student and family needs. They represent the school to the news media. And they celebrate the school's accomplishments publicly.

Leaders recognize that the school is a public institution. They invite community members to hold classes for adults in the building, or open health facilities to members of the community as well as students. Such efforts extend school resources to the community, and are increasingly necessary in tight fiscal environments.

Leaders see their constituency as the whole community, not just the parents of students in schools. In many communities, a large majority of taxpayers do not have children in schools and need to be convinced of the need to support education. By serving as community leaders, principals help persuade these adults that the next generation of leaders is in school and needs the best quality education to take on these leadership roles.

Leaders also advocate for schools. Like ministers, business leaders, public officials and local elected leaders, principals have a voice to speak out for children, education funding, services, commitments, resources and policy that affect teaching and learning. When additional resources or policy changes to support the school's goals are needed, effective school leaders step forward and make the case for why the changes would improve student learning or administrative operations.

1 Learning Centered
2 Diverse Communities
3 21st Century Learners
4 Quality Instruction
5 Knowledge and Data
6 Community Engagement

## INSIDE A SCHOOL: A FOCUS ON PRACTICE

**Kaneohe Elementary School, Kaneohe, Hawaii**
**Principal Mitchell Otani**

As in real estate, location means everything in partnership. Kaneohe Elementary is a mile from the on-ramp to a highway that links a naval air base to Pearl Harbor, so when an officer from the air base drove by the school in the late 1990s, he thought it would make a perfect partner. And that was just fine with Mitchell Otani, Kaneohe's principal, who had been looking for a military partner since a marine unit moved away a few years before.

Over the past few years, sailors from the naval station have helped the school with physical education, provided tutoring for students, built benches on the school grounds and helped with campus beautification. "You can get a lot of things from one person driving by," Otani says.

The school has had a similarly good relationship with the carpenter union, which lent apprentices to build a storage facility for the school. Normally, the facility would have cost $70,000, but Kaneohe had to pay only $6,000 for the materials.

To Otani, such partnerships are essential. "In a day of tight budgets, schools can't do it alone anymore," he says. But beyond the financial benefits, partnerships have also helped build good will in the community, which has also benefited his school. Enrollment grew by about 50 percent, to 600, in the 1990s and has remained at that level ever since. And the school draws students from a wide area, not just in its immediate zone, Otani notes, because of its reputation for excellence.

"It makes good sense to enlist all the resources of the community, and parents," he says.

1 Learning Centered

2 Diverse Communities

3 21st Century Learners

4 Quality Instruction

5 Knowledge and Data

6 Community Engagement

## Shape partnerships to ensure multiple learning opportunities for students, in and out of school

To help accomplish school goals, leaders form partnerships with community organizations, business and industry, foundations and public agencies to extend student learning within and beyond the school day. Leaders recognize that schools alone cannot educate students to high levels and that learning takes place in a variety of settings. Post-secondary education, businesses, cultural organizations and families offer financial and material resources that can support instruction. Bringing such outside groups into schools can bolster public support.

For example, leaders form partnerships that offer students the opportunity to visit workplaces to see how academic knowledge and skills are applied. They build connections to enable children to use city facilities for after-school programs. They create links with preschool providers and parents to increase student learning and development. They attract resources to enable teachers to participate in professional development opportunities provided by community organizations. Such opportunities also help develop broader outcomes for students. When schools make connections to community facilities, for example, students have more opportunities to receive social, physical and mental health services.

The public and the education community agree strongly on the need for some type of organized activity or place for children to go after school every day. Nearly three-in-four parents say that after-school programs are an "absolute necessity" in their communities. More than three-fourths of elementary school principals whose schools offer after-school programs say it is "extremely important" to maintain these programs. More than at any time in the past, Americans recognize that after-school programs help children learn, keep them safe and help working families.

Elementary school principals have the best vantage point for observing how many children start school unprepared and how their delayed learning influences their school success. As leaders of the critical first years of public schooling, elementary principals need to take full advantage of every opportunity to define for parents and the community the importance of school readiness—the skills or stages of development of a five-year-old entering kindergarten. In making this effort to link early childhood learning to the broader education spectrum, principals must reach deeper into the community.

These types of collaborative partnerships reinforce principals' roles as community leaders. They also strengthen community support for the schools by informing community leaders about schools. Such information helps dispel stereotypes and provides community members a view of the challenges principals face and the ways they are meeting them.

## A CLOSER LOOK

### Increasing Family and Community Involvement

Family and community involvement is key to improving student achievement. The Commissioner's Parents Advisory Council of Kentucky developed these six objectives to increase parent and community leadership:

1. **Relationship-building.** The school staff builds productive, personal relationships with parents of all students.

2. **Communications.** Two-way information in many forms flows regularly between school staff and parents about students' academic achievement and individual needs.

3. **Decision-making.** School staff encourages, supports and expects parents to be involved in school improvement decisions and to monitor and assist school improvement.

4. **Advocacy.** For each student, the school staff identifies and supports a parent or other adult who can take personal responsibility for understanding and speaking for that child's learning needs.

5. **Learning opportunities.** The school staff ensures that families have multiple opportunities to understand how to support their children's learning.

6. **Community partnerships.** The school staff engages and partners with community members to plan and implement substantive work to improve student achievement.

Source: Commissioner's Parents Advisory Council of Kentucky. *The Missing Piece of the Proficiency Puzzle.* Frankfort, KY: Kentucky Department of Education, June 2007.

See Appendix 1 for the *Kentucky Family and Community Involvement Guide to Student Achievement.*

## Market the school's distinctive learning environment and results to inform parents' choices of options that best fit their children's needs

As school leaders, principals are the public faces of their schools. Leaders represent schools at community events and in meetings with community organizations, as well as in informal settings, like backyard barbecues and trips to the mall. They speak openly to the news media to describe school programs and achievements. By showing schools' accomplishments and being visible in the community, principals can build support for their schools.

As school programs become more diverse to meet the needs of their diverse student populations, principals have an increasing responsibility to provide information on the distinctiveness of the school's programs and its accomplishments. By speaking in public forums and providing materials to parents and community members, principals are marketing their schools and making a case for their success.

Such efforts are particularly important in districts where parents can choose among public schools. Parents need information to make sound decisions, and effective leaders make information widely available to ensure that parents can match a school program with their children's needs.

Parental choice in education includes a number of policy options that enable parents to choose the best schools for their children. Depending on the policies of a state or system, choice options include:

- Charter schools, which appear in 40 states and the District of Columbia

- Public school choice, within or between districts, which includes magnet schools and is guaranteed in 15 states

- Tuition vouchers and scholarships, which exist in seven states

- Dual enrollment programs that exist in 38 states, 18 of which have mandatory programs that allow qualifying high school students to attend college classes and receive higher education credits

- Home schooling, which is legal in all states

The growing prevalence of choice requires principals to pay more attention to their "customers." Joseph Murphy, professor of education at the Peabody School of Education at Vanderbilt University, says, "For 150 years, there has been a public monopoly on education and people looked to government to provide services. That has since broken. We're moving from a producer system to a customer/client system. That system causes you to lead schools very differently—it's very different than the old bureaucratic ways. One principal in New York would take parents on tours of the school; the next year she had 100 one-hour tours lined up. If she didn't market her school, she wouldn't have one. There are some serious implications on how principals do their business. We haven't been a customer-sensitive kind of business. I think those days are over. If parents want a Montessori school, you'd better create one."

1 Learning Centered

2 Diverse Communities

3 21st Century Learners

4 Quality Instruction

5 Knowledge and Data

6 Community Engagement

## Advocate for high-quality education for every student

Principals are key allies in organizing for equity at the community, state and federal levels. Principals' relationships with parents and community members help in these organizing efforts. Working with parents and others in the community, principals can help to broker resources at the local, state and federal levels that help to achieve equity in public education.

When advocating for all children, principals face challenges that are both tangible—most common is the issue of funding—and intangible, such as competing values.

**Balance of choice and equity.** Americans increasingly want the opportunity to choose from among a diverse array of school options. At the same time, Americans strongly believe that all children should learn at high levels. These two values, choice and equity, can conflict. Unrestrained school choice could result in situations that are highly inequitable, if some schools attract only advantaged students while others continue to educate those with the greatest needs. And these situations can set up conflicts over resources because children with the greatest needs require more resources.

Principals can lead communities through these dilemmas by helping define the proper balance between these potentially competing, yet equally important, values. And they can advocate for equitable funding to ensure that every child has the resources needed to achieve high levels of learning.

**Funding.** Despite the growing consensus on the need to raise achievement for all students, the likelihood of dramatic increases in funding for education remains slim for the foreseeable future. The strong opposition to large tax increases combined with commitments to other social needs such as health care suggest that schools are not likely to see dramatic increases in financial resources in the coming decades. In addition, changes in other aspects of society, such as the aging of the Baby Boom generation, mean that the competition for funding might get even more intense.

The long-term strategy is to organize a campaign to support significant increases in funding for schools over time. Education remains a top priority, and support is more likely if the community sees results that match its interest. That strategy can be supported by the school leader's consistent attention to making the most of the revenues that do exist. Using whatever expertise they can muster, principals need to scour district, school and community budgets to ensure that all available funds support improved learning that prepares all students for the 21st century.

# INSIDE A SCHOOL: A FOCUS ON PRACTICE

**Yvonne T. McKitrick Elementary School, Lutz, Florida**
**Principal Lisa Yost**

Every year, McKitrick Elementary holds a celebratory breakfast for members of the "110% Club." To join, a parent or community member must volunteer at least 110 hours a year at the school. Last year, nearly 40 people joined by tutoring, serving as chaperones, reading to classes, helping in the media center and performing a variety of other duties. Many of the club's members logged far more than 110 hours; overall, parents and community members have volunteered more than 20,000 hours a year.

Lisa Yost, McKitrick's principal since the school opened in 2001, says parent involvement began even before the school opened its doors. Parents set up the furniture, chose the school colors, stacked books in the library and helped get the school ready to open. "We wanted to invite people in and make them part of their children's education," Yost says.

To Yost, parent and community involvement is an essential ingredient in school success. "I strongly believe that when parents are involved with their children's education, children perform better, academically and socially," she says.

McKitrick also returns the favor by getting involved in the community. The school has a close relationship with the Tampa Players theater group, located across the street, and McKitrick has "adopted" a school from a disadvantaged area of the district.

By opening its doors to parents and the community, McKitrick has built support for the school, Yost notes. When parents and community members visit the school, they see teachers who put in 110 percent as well. "They can have confidence sending their children here," she says. "It makes you the best school you can be."

1 Learning Centered

2 Diverse Communities

3 21st Century Learners

4 Quality Instruction

5 Knowledge and Data

6 Community Engagement

**Standard 6:** Reflection Questions

1. How can engagement with community leaders be strengthened so all community resources that support students and their families are aligned in ways that better support learning and development?

2. Are the messages the school staff communicates to the community consistent about student learning needs and accomplishments? Are these messages communicated in the language and culture of each stakeholder group to reduce the number of disenfranchised parents and community members?

3. What are the best indicators that show a school community is engaged in shared accountability for all students' learning?

4. How can the increased regularity of interaction and involvement of diverse parents and community members in every aspect of public education—planning, teaching, support services, evaluation—improve student and adult learning?

5. How can the voting percentages of school staff, parents and community members be increased to support public education finances and resources?

6. How can student and adult learning successes be celebrated by the school community and engage everyone in taking action on needed improvements?

7. How can partnerships with community organizations, agencies and educational institutions create teaching and learning environments that blur the line between student learning in and out of school?

8. How can the number of advocates for public education be increased by creating in-person, electronic and print platforms for their voices to become an ongoing part of the community dialogue?

# Standard 6: Action Steps

After answering the Reflection Questions, list the Action Steps needed to attain the learning goals specific to each question:

| Reflection Question | Action Step(s) | Who needs to take the lead?<br>Who needs to be involved? |
|---|---|---|
| 1 | | |
| 2 | | |
| 3 | | |
| 4 | | |
| 5 | | |
| 6 | | |
| 7 | | |
| 8 | | |

**Standard 6:** Leadership Continuum

This self-assessment continuum is intended to help you move toward higher levels of leadership. Consider using this tool at the beginning of the school year and again at the end to assess areas of growth and to identify needed areas of personal and behavioral change.

| Strategy | Level 1 | Level 2 | Level 3 | Level 4 | Level 5 | Score Circle One |
|---|---|---|---|---|---|---|
| **1. Engage parents, families and the community to build relationships that support improved performance.** | There is no system for engaging diverse people to improve performance. | Parents from diverse backgrounds are usually involved in the school through formal structures required by local, state, national or federal mandates. | The principal, teacher leaders and some parents, regardless of home language or background, are invited to be involved in the school, primarily supporting administrative tasks or athletic, social or academic events. | The principal and teachers seek input from all parents and families to create meaningful engagement that supports student performance. Parent, family and community engagement targets are set and achieved. | The principal, teachers and involved volunteers regularly engage with stakeholders to expand relationships and participation. Data about participation and student performance is compared with effective engagement programs and practices in the nation. | 1 2 3 4 5 |
| **2. Serve as civic leaders who regularly engage with numerous stakeholders to support students, families and schools in more effective ways.** | The principal has no active leadership role within the community. | The principal reports to the community and media on the progress of student achievement as required by local, state, national or federal mandates. | The principal is not viewed as a civic leader, but periodically informs the school community about programs and needed resources to support events or special programs. | The principal represents the school community on some local family and student issues beyond education, and encourages teachers to be public voices for the school and connect community services to students and families. | The community recognizes the principal as an active, collaborative civic leader. The principal and many teachers and some staff are visible participants in community efforts identifying, advocating and securing supports for students and families. | 1 2 3 4 5 |

| Strategy | Level 1 | Level 2 | Level 3 | Level 4 | Level 5 | Score Circle One |
|---|---|---|---|---|---|---|
| **3. Shape partnerships to ensure multiple learning opportunities for students, in and out of school.** | There are no partnerships, alliances or coalitions with agencies, community organizations, foundations and businesses in the community to support student or adult learning. | A few school and community partnerships exist because of local, state, national or federal mandates. | The principal actively shapes in-school partnerships that vary widely in topics, investment of resources and expected results. | The principal and many teachers regularly scan the interests and resources of different sectors of the community to establish learning partnerships explicitly aligned with the learning needs of students with an increased emphasis on out-of-school experiences. | The principal, most teachers and some staff work collaboratively with the community to create, align and sustain a partnership system of in-school and out-of-school learning experiences accessible to all students. | 1 2 3 4 5 |
| **4. Market the school's distinctive learning environment and results to inform parents' choices of options that best fit their children's needs.** | The school has no distinctive learning environment. A list of the school's programs and results is available on request. | Parents are notified of new programs and results are reported as required by local, state, national and federal mandates. | The principal, counselors and teacher leaders inform parents about unique or varied instructional choices. | The principal, counselors and most teachers market and explain the school's unique learning opportunities to students and parents to jointly determine the best fit. | The principal, counselors, teachers, students and parents market the school and its uniqueness to the entire community, and everyone shares responsibility for determining the best fit. | 1 2 3 4 5 |
| **5. Advocate for high-quality education for every student** | There is no proactive community engagement or advocacy in policymaking or legislation about public schools. | The principal invites specific parents and community leaders to speak to policymakers or legislators when the superintendent or school board request or approve such input. | The principal encourages some parents and community leaders to speak out about school and district policies. | The principal and some teachers reach out to educate parents and some community members about economic and political needs of the school or district. | The principal and many teachers regularly work collaboratively with parents and community leaders to educate and advocate for funding support for public education, policies and legislation that support learning for every student. | 1 2 3 4 5 |

1 Learning Centered

2 Diverse Communities

3 21st Century Learners

4 Quality Instruction

5 Knowledge and Data

6 Community Engagement

# For More Information

## Resources from NAESP

In the 2006 publication, *Leading After-School Learning Communities*, NAESP outlined six standards for principals who leverage learning and community resources for learning. This publication gives principals the knowledge, tools and resources to lead and actively promote, establish, operate, evaluate and sustain quality after-school programs.

Elementary school principals have a big job that keeps getting bigger, but the bottom line remains providing young children the knowledge and skills they will need to succeed in school and in life. In *Leading Early Childhood Learning Communities* (2005), NAESP identifies six standards for what principals should know and be able to do as leaders of early childhood learning communities.

*Spotlight on Promising Practices: Stories of Principals Actively Engaging Communities* (3rd Edition, 2007) is part of NAESP's Sharing the Dream project, which enables principals to test ideas on how to involve and engage their communities. In these efforts, principals build greater ownership for the work of the school by sharing leadership and decision-making among various community members and creating strong learning communities.

## On the Web

**Resources on Afterschool** (www.afterschoolresources.org), created by Collaborative Communications Group, is an online tool that contains information on after-school research and evaluation, promising practices, professional development, public awareness and communications, policy and financing.

**The Coalition for Community Schools** (www.communityschools.org) advocates for community schools as the vehicle for strengthening schools, families and communities. A variety of resources for sustaining community schools, as well as a list of national models, are available on this site.

**The Harvard Family Research Project** features a section on complementary learning (www.gse.harvard.edu/hfrp/projects/complementary-learning.html). Resources are offered on the best ways to build family support for programs, how to leverage support for after-school programs among community organizations, how to best support parents with early childhood development and much more.

## Resources and Research

**Sexton, R.** *Mobilizing Citizens for Better Schools.* **New York: Teachers College Press, 2004.**

This book provides ideas for all citizens who are interested in school reform. It covers initial organizing, building credibility, working with business and the media, navigating the ins and outs of school reform, organizing the public and communication strategies.

**Collaborative Communications Group.** *New Relationships with Schools: Organizations That Build Community by Connecting With Schools.* **Volume IV. Washington, D.C.: Collaborative Communications Group, 2007.**

This is the fourth report in a series that takes a look at the success of organizations that build community by connecting with schools. Volume IV analyzes how conversation-based engagement efforts can benefit the community and identifies lessons learned that could help other communities working to strengthen local support for schools.

# Shared Leadership and Accountability: A Call to Action

**I**f school leaders are to meet the challenges that transformations in leadership, society and education will create for student and adult learning, they will require stronger preparation, enhanced professional development and additional resources at a number of levels. These supports demand shared leadership and accountability not just in schools—but also in the federal government, states and districts, as well as in post-secondary institutions, school systems and communities. Together with principals, these agencies and organizations share responsibility for student learning and development. Collectively, they must be accountable for the success of all students.

**Here are 10 ways that school districts, states, the federal government and universities can share leadership and accountability with principals:**

School districts can:

1. **Build principals' capacity to provide instructional leadership.** Principals must have time and resources to develop the knowledge and skills they need to lead high-performance schools, as well as the resources to function effectively as instructional leaders in their buildings. Time for professional development can help equip school leaders with additional knowledge, and professional learning support directed at their instructional needs can enhance their knowledge and skills. At the same time, principals need professional development to help them understand how to lead, manage and support learning communities—such as interaction with peers at state and national conferences and technological resources to stay connected with their peers—to enable them to form networks with other schools and disseminate information within the school community. Such support should begin on the first day of the job, with a skilled mentor to guide a principal through a successful transition into his or her new position, and should continue with coaching throughout a principal's tenure.

2. **Provide support, funding and flexibility for alternative leadership arrangements.** For principals to perform their instructional leadership functions effectively, they need to share the management functions of the school. In some places, schools and districts are creating new positions to take on some of those responsibilities. But assistant principals, lead teachers and guidance counselors can also lead functions that can enable principals to focus on instructional leadership. More research is needed in defining how these alternative management structures might work. And districts can model these arrangements by creating leadership teams in the central office that enable "chief academic officers" to focus on instructional leadership and "chief management officers" to focus on operations.

3. **Improve working conditions.** One of the most serious challenges facing the profession is a shortage of applicants. Fewer people are seeking to become principals, in part because many fear that principals are increasingly held accountable for school results without the authority and support they need to produce results. Principals need autonomy over budgets and hiring to create and maintain school programs that match school goals, and financial support from districts to serve their student populations effectively.

4. **Improve salaries and pay structures.** School leaders deserve salaries commensurate with other professionals with similar responsibilities. And, like other professionals, they should earn financial rewards for effectiveness and should be able to advance in their careers. States and districts should establish incentives for principals to meet standards and should provide rewards, such as sabbaticals, advanced training and international exchanges, for successful leaders.

5. **Assess principals fairly.** Principals are—and should be—accountable for improving student achievement, but evaluations of principals should consider a range of measures of their performance, not just standardized test scores. Progress toward school performance targets and the standards included in *Leading Learning Communities* should be measured as well. Principals do have expertise and skills that can be measured. However, these measurements can be highly subjective and easily misinterpreted. Attention must be paid to defining and disseminating what we know to be effective in the profession and championing the "whole school leader."

States can:

6. **Refine and strengthen data collection.** Under the No Child Left Behind Act, districts can replace principals of schools in restructuring status. While principals are rightly accountable for their school's performance, accountability should be more than an all-or-nothing proposition. Accountability should come with additional resources that enable schools to build the capacity needed to meet agreed-upon goals. These resources can be conditional; if the school does not improve, the state can step in and take over the management of the school.

An accurate grasp of the current situation in American public schools is possible only with the use of longitudinal data. Data that tracks students from elementary school to college allows researchers to analyze trends in education, both good and bad. Only by increasing the type of data collected over time will policymakers ever have the accurate information they need to address educational issues in a timely fashion.

7. **Build learning opportunities and networks of principals.** To enable principals to build learning communities, and to end their traditional isolation, states and districts should create opportunities for principals to meet and collaborate with their peers in other schools and districts. These opportunities can include conferences, electronic networks and Listservs, and coaching and mentoring.

The federal government can:

8. **Support a voluntary advanced certification system for principals.** Principals should be recognized and rewarded for their excellence in the profession and commitment to their own growth and development. We have advocated for a comprehensive review process in which principals demonstrate their skills, expertise and the art of the profession.

A national certification process, similar to the one developed by the National Board for Professional Teaching Standards, would not only reward effective principals, but it would also set a target for improvement for all principals and provide a guide for professional development. The certification system should include the *Leading Learning Communities* standards and other benchmarks as defined by practitioners and other leaders in the field. The federal government should fund it.

9. **Develop federal programs that strengthen principals' ability to serve all students.** The No Child Left Behind Act placed too little emphasis on the critical role of principals in enhancing student achievement. While the law rightly focused on highly qualified teachers, it did little to create incentives or provide support for recruiting and retaining effective principals.

   In addition, funding for the law has never matched authorized levels, leaving schools with too few resources to meet the challenging standards it sets. Nor has Congress ever come close to funding the Individuals with Disabilities Education Act (IDEA) at the level originally authorized. By increasing funding for these and other programs, the federal government can help districts support principals through mentoring and other professional development efforts, while holding them accountable for results.

Colleges and universities can:

10. **Redesign principal and teacher preparation programs.** Principal and teacher preparation increasingly takes place in diverse settings—in universities, in district-run programs, in programs created by private organizations—and learning takes place in a variety of ways. Regardless of the setting or format, principal preparation programs should be guided by the *Leading Learning Communities* standards. However principals get to their jobs, they will be leading learning communities.

   Preparation programs have not kept pace with changes in schools, and too often do not adequately equip future principals with the knowledge and skills they need. And few programs are designed to prepare principals for the challenges they will face in the coming decade. Principals need programs that focus on instructional leadership; knowledge and use of technology; understanding of collaborative learning environments; collaborative and distributed leadership skills; cultural competence; ability to work with multiple data sources and accountability measures; and understanding of the complex needs of children—academic and social, physical and emotional—if they are to succeed in the 21st century.

   Teacher and administrative preparation programs should also be redesigned to support building the capacity of everyone to work effectively in learning communities and align their efforts to schoolwide improvement goals. These programs should also address the skills that students need in the new century and the diversity of the student population. Teacher and administrator preparation programs should collect information from graduates and their supervisors to monitor their effectiveness in increasing student and adult learning.

# Methodology:
# A Conversation
# by, of and for Principals

**T**he National Association of Elementary School Principals and Collaborative Communications Group first worked together in 2001 to produce the landmark publication *Leading Learning Communities: Standards for What Principals Should Know and Be Able To Do*, which created standards for principal performance. In 2007, NAESP again asked Collaborative Communications to conduct a rigorous examination of research; to engage principals, researchers and individuals in professional organizations concerned with leading learning communities; and to write and design the updated and expanded second edition of *Leading Learning Communities: Standards for What Principals Should Know and Be Able To Do*.

The process was designed to:

- **Engage NAESP members in defining quality in schools and revisiting and revising the standards for school leaders**

- **Identify and illuminate effective practices aligned with the principal standards**

- **Review drafts of the guide in relation to NAESP's strategic direction and for authenticity in relation to the practice of principals**

- **Use the updated and expanded standards guide as a vehicle to encourage all principals to reflect on their practice**

The 10-month process included:

**Discovery interviews.** Thought leaders in research, policy, practice and leadership provided significant perspective regarding the changes of the profession and the role that NAESP can play in helping to navigate this new territory.

**Interviews with NAESP staff.** NAESP's executive leadership team provided critical insights on the need for, and structure and content of, this guide.

**Creation and convening of a Standards Committee.** A representative group of principals, nominated by NAESP State Leaders, met in October, December and January to outline, discuss and review this guide. Throughout the process, the committee also participated in an online learning community via a Listserv to share reflections. Mary Kay Sommers, the president of NAESP, chaired the committee.

**Scholarly research.** A review of relevant research spanned education and organizational leadership and management, instructional practice, academic standards, developments in data and public engagement.

**Discussion with the NAESP Board of Directors.** The January 2008 board meeting provided an opportunity for reflection on the draft and fundamental messages of the guide and standards.

**Review of drafts.** In addition to reviews by the NAESP staff and Standards Committee, past NAESP presidents, the Resolutions Committee, state executives and other professionals who work closely with principals provided candid and invaluable feedback that helped to ensure accuracy, credibility and relevance.

## Committee on Standards for Principals

NAESP gratefully acknowledges the contributions of the representatives from each of the regional zones and others on the committee for their tireless energy and thoughtful reflection on the complex role of the principal.

**Mary Kay Sommers**
Committee Chair
NAESP President
Principal
Shepardson Elementary School
Fort Collins, CO

**Martha Albers**
Principal
Hilbert Elementary School
Sherwood, WI

**Mary Booker**
Principal
Francis Scott Key Elementary School
Baltimore, MD

**Gretchen Donndelinger**
Administrator and Program Professor
Nova Southeastern University
Fischler School of Education and Human Services
Carlsbad, CA

**Angelina Finnegan**
Principal
Rockaway Meadow Elementary School
Parsippany, NJ

**Katherine Grondin**
Principal
Sherwood Heights School
Auburn, ME

**Lucretia Jackson**
Principal
Maury Elementary School
Alexandria, VA

**Sharon Knudson**
Principal
Jessup Elementary School
Cheyenne, WA

**Carol Miller**
Principal
McFerran School
Louisville, KY

**Bernadette Nevarez**
Albuquerque Public Schools
West Mesa Cluster Leader
Albuquerque, NM

**Todd Williford**
Principal
Sallie Zetterower Elementary School
Statesboro, GA

**Byron Yankey**
Principal
Frontier Elementary School
Boise, ID

## Acknowledgments

Developing the second edition of *Leading Learning Communities: Standards for What Principals Should Know and Be Able To Do* was a collaborative process synthesizing research, personal reflections and collective wisdom. NAESP gratefully acknowledges the people who contributed to this effort, including:

- The many principals—aspiring, new, veteran and retired—who generously shared their stories and whose passion challenges us all to remember the children.

- Executive directors of NAESP State Affiliates and the many principals who serve as State Leaders, for their deep commitment to the work of our professional associations.

- The key leaders and researchers who took part in the discovery interviews on the future role of the principal, including:

**Walter Bender**, President for Software and Content Development
One Laptop per Child

**Jo Blase**, Professor of Educational Leadership
University of Georgia

**Milton Chen**, Executive Director
George Lucas Education Foundation

**Richard DuFour**
School Improvement Consultant

**Michael Fullan**, Professor Emeritus of Education
Ontario Institute for Studies in Education

**Steve Heck**, Executive Director
Indiana Association of School Principals

**Nadya Aswad Higgins**, Executive Director
Massachusetts Elementary School Principals Association

**Jason Leahy**, Executive Director
Illinois Principals Association

**Joseph Murphy**, Professor of Education
Peabody College of Education, Vanderbilt University

**H. Wells Singleton**, Education Provost and University Dean
Fischler School of Education and Human Services, Nova Southeastern University

**James Spillane**, Professor
School of Education and Social Policy, Northwestern University

**Tom Welch**, Consultant
International Center for Leadership in Education

- James L. Doud, NAESP Past-President (1984-85), for his ongoing counsel and support in the development of the NAESP Standards.

- NAESP staff, for their commitment to providing research, professional development and expanded learning opportunities for elementary and middle school principals across the country.

- Collaborative Communications Group staff and consultants for their shared belief in the process of collaboration and for their commitment to updating and expanding this guide with the latest research and newest tools and resources available, including Kris Kurtenbach and Terri Ferinde Dunham, Partners; Celia Alicata; Gloria Frazier; Bill Glover; Lori Meyer; Ellen Parker; and Robert Rothman.

NAESP also acknowledges the NAESP Board of Directors, listed below, for their commitment to calling for progressive practice and high-quality learning opportunities for all children.

# Additional Resources

## Standard One: Lead Student and Adult Learning

Brafman, O., and R. Beckstrom. *The Starfish and the Spider: The Unstoppable Power of Leaderless Organizations*. New York: Portfolio, 2006.

Carasso, A., C. E. Steuerle and G. Reynolds. *Kids' Share 2007: How Children Fare in the Federal Budget*. Washington, D.C. : Urban Institute, 2007.

Collins, J. *Good to Great and the Social Sectors: A Monograph to Accompany Good to Great*. New York: HarperCollins, 2005.

Collins, J. *Good to Great: Why Some Companies Make the Leap . . . and Others Don't*. New York: HarperBusiness, 2001.

DuFour, R. "Beyond Instructional Leadership: The Learning-Centered Principal." *Educational Leadership*. Vol. 59, No. 8. Alexandria, VA: Association for Supervision and Curriculum Development, 2002.

Institute for Alternative Futures (IAF). *Provocative Forecasts of Uncertainty and Opportunity: A 2021 Dialogue on Schools & the Principalship*. Alexandria, VA: IAF, 2006.

Institute for Alternative Futures. *Anticipating the Future of Schools and the Principalship*. Alexandria, VA: IAF, 2006.

Leithwood, K., and C. Riehl. *What Do We Already Know About Successful School Leadership?* Washington, D.C. : American Educational Research Association (AERA) Division A, 2003.

Martin, A. *The Changing Nature of Leadership.* Greensboro, NC: Center for Creative Leadership, 2006.

MetLife. *The MetLife Survey of the American Teacher: An Examination of School Leadership.* New York: MetLife, 2003.

Public Agenda. *Rolling Up Their Sleeves: Superintendents and Principals Talk About What's Needed to Fix Public Schools.* Washington, D.C. : Public Agenda, 2003.

Rosborg, J., M. McGee and J. Burgett. *What Every Superintendent and Principal Needs to Know.* Novato, CA: Education Communication Unlimited, 2007.

Samuels, C. A. "Managers Help Principals Balance Time." *Education Week.* February 11, 2008 (online), February 13, 2008 (print).

School Leadership for the 21st Century Initiative. *Leadership for Student Learning: Reinventing the Principalship.* Washington, D.C. : Institute of Educational Leadership, 2000.

Senge, P. *The Fifth Discipline: The Art & Practice of the Learning Organization.* Revised Edition. New York: Currency, 2006.

Spillane, J., and J. Diamond. *Distributed Leadership in Practice.* New York: Teachers College Press, 2007.

Waters, T., R. Marzano and B. McNulty. *Balanced Leadership: What 30 Years of Research Tells Us About the Effect of Leadership on Student Achievement.* Aurora, CO: McREL, 2003.

Whittle, C. *Crash Course: Imagining a Better Future for Public Education.* New York: Riverhead Books, 2005.

Whittle, C., and H. Levin. "Forum: Our Schools in the Year 2030: How Will They Be Different?" *Education Next.* Vol. 6, No. 2. Stanford, CA: Hoover Institution, 2006.

Williams, J. "Breaking the Mold: How Do School Entrepreneurs Create Change?" *Education Next.* Vol. 6, No. 2. Stanford, CA: Hoover Institution, 2006.

## Standard Two: Lead Diverse Communities

Blank, M., and A. Berg. *All Together Now: Sharing Responsibility for the Whole Child*. Alexandria, VA: Association for Supervision and Curriculum Development, 2006.

Bordas, J. *Salsa, Soul, and Spirit: Leadership for Multicultural Age*. San Francisco: Berrett-Koehler, 2007.

Garcia, E. *Teaching and Learning in Two Languages: Bilingualism and Schooling in the United States*. New York: Teachers College Press, 2005.

Hodgkinson, H. *The Whole Child in a Fractured World*. Alexandria, VA: Association for Curriculum and Supervision Development, 2006.

Lee, V., and D. Burkam. *Inequality at the Starting Gate: Social Background Differences in Achievement as Children Begin School*. Washington, D.C. : Economic Policy Institute, 2002.

Matthews, H., and D. Ewen. *Reaching All Children? Understanding Early Care and Education Participation Among Immigrant Families*. Washington, D.C. : Center for Law and Social Policy, 2006.

New Visions for Public Schools. "Ten Principles of Effective School Design." New York: New Visions for Public Schools, 2006.

Pankratz, R., and J. Petrosko, eds. *All Children Can Learn: Lessons from the Kentucky Reform Experience*. San Francisco: Jossey-Bass, 2000.

Pink, D. *A Whole New Mind: Why Right-Brainers Will Rule the Future*. New York: Riverhead Trade, 2006.

Singleton, G. E., and C. Linton. *Courageous Conversations About Race: A Field Guide for Achieving Equity in Schools*. Thousand Oaks, CA: Corwin Press, 2005.

Thomas, W., and V. Collier. *A National Study of School Effectiveness for Language Minority Students' Long-Term Academic Achievement Final Report: Project 1.1*. Berkeley, CA: Center for Research on Education, Diversity & Excellence, 2002.

Tilly, W. D. "Response to Intervention: What Is It? Why Do It? Is It Worth It?" *The Special Edge*. Vol. 19, No. 2. Sacramento, CA: California Department of Education's Special Education Division, 2007.

### Standard Three: Lead 21st Century Learning

Adamowski, S., S. Bowles Therriault and A. Cavanna. *The Autonomy Gap: Barriers to Effective School Leadership*. Washington, D.C. : American Institutes for Research and Thomas B. Fordham Institute, 2007.

Blankstein, A., R. Cole and P. Houston, eds. *The Soul of Educational Leadership Series*. Thousand Oaks, CA: Corwin Press, 2006–2008.

Education Week. *Leading for Learning*. Bethesda, MD: Editorial Projects in Education, 2004, 2005, 2006 and 2007.

Fischler School of Education and Human Services. *Innovate: Journal of Online Education*.Fort Lauderdale-Davie, FL: Nova Southeastern University, bimonthly. Available at: http://www.innovateonline.info

Friedman, T. L. *The World Is Flat: A Brief History of the Twenty-First Century*. New York: Farrar, Straus and Giroux, 2006.

The George Lucas Educational Foundation. *Edutopia: Success Stories for Learning in the Digital Age*. San Francisco: Jossey-Bass, 2002.

Kauerz, K. "State Kindergarten Policies: Straddling Early Learning and Early Elementary School." *Young Children*. Vol. 60, No. 2. Washington, D.C. : National Association for the Education of Young Children, 2005.

Leithwood, K., K. Seashore Louis, S. Anderson and K. Wahlstrom. *How Leadership Influences Student Learning*. New York: The Wallace Foundation, 2004.

Lockwood, A. T. *The Principal's Guide to Afterschool Programs*. Thousand Oaks, CA: Corwin Press, 2007.

McMurrer, J. *Choices, Changes, and Challenges: Curriculum and Instruction in the NCLB Era*. Washington, D.C. : Center on Education Policy, 2007.

New Commission on the Skills of the American Workforce. *Tough Choices or Tough Times: Executive Summary*. Washington, D.C. : National Center on Education and the Economy, 2007.

Pink, D. "School's Out: Get Ready for the New Age of Individualized Education." *Reason Online*. Los Angeles: Reason, 2001.

Pitler, H., E. Hubbell, M. Kuhn and K. Malenoski. *Using Technology With Classroom Instruction That Works*. Alexandria, VA: Association for Supervision and Curriculum Development, 2007.

Prensky, M. *Don't Bother Me Mom—I'm Learning!* St. Paul, MN: Paragon House Publishers, 2006.

Rotherham, A. J. *Hard Wiring: What the Next Decade in Education Policy Means for Educational Technology*. Washington, D.C. : Education Sector, 2005.

School Leadership for the 21st Century Initiative. *Leadership for Student Learning: Reinventing the Principalship*. Washington, D.C. : Institute for Educational Leadership, 2000.

Shaffer, D. W. *How Computer Games Help Children Learn*. New York, NY: Palgrave Macmillan, 2006.

Spillane, J. "Primary School Leadership Practice: How the Subject Matters." *School Leadership and Management*. Vol. 25, No. 4. New York: Routledge, 2005.

Supovitz, J., and S. Poglinco. *Instructional Leadership in a Standards-Based Reform*. Philadelphia, PA: Consortium for Policy Research in Education, 2001.

Tapscott, D., and A. D. Williams. *Wikinomics: How Mass Collaboration Changes Everything*. New York: Portfolio, 2006.

## Standard Four: Lead Continuous Improvement

Adams, Jr., J., and M. Copland. *When Learning Counts: Rethinking Licenses for School Leaders*. Seattle, WA: Center on Reinventing Public Education, University of Washington, 2005.

Blase, J., and J. Blase. *Teachers Bringing Out the Best in Teachers: A Guide to Peer Consultation for Administrators and Teachers*. Thousand Oaks, CA: Corwin Press, 2006.

Block, P. *The Answer to How Is Yes: Acting on What Matters*. San Francisco: Berrett-Koehler Publishers, 2006.

Conrad, L., and K. Hupfeld. *From Surviving to Thriving: Strategies for Success in a High-Stakes Accountability System*. Denver, CO: Public Education & Business Coalition, 2006.

Council of Chief State School Officers (CCSSO). *Interstate School Leaders Licensure Consortium: Standards for School Leaders*. Washington, D.C. : CCSSO, 1996.

Darling-Hammond, L., M. LaPointe, D. Meyerson and M. Orr. *Preparing School Leaders for a Changing World: Lessons From Exemplary Leadership Development Programs*. Stanford, CA: Stanford Educational Leadership Institute, Stanford University, 2007.

Davis, Stephen, L. Darling-Hammond, M. LaPointe and D. Meyerson. *School Leadership Study: Developing Successful Principals*. Stanford, CA: Stanford Educational Leadership Institute, Stanford University, 2005.

Eaker, R., R. DuFour and R. Burnette. *Getting Started: Reculturing Schools to Become Professional Learning Communities*. Bloomington, IN: Solution Tree, 2002.

Fullan, M. "Change the Terms for Teacher Learning." *Journal of Staff Development*. Vol. 28, No. 3. Oxford, OH: National Staff Development Council, 2007.

Gray, C., B. Fry, G. Bottoms and K. O'Neil. Good *Principals Aren't Born—They're Mentored: Are We Investing Enough to Get the School Leaders We Need?* Atlanta, GA: Southern Regional Education Board, 2007.

Hess, F., and A. Kelly. "The Accidental Principal: What Doesn't Get Taught at Ed Schools?" *Education Next*. Vol. 5, No. 3. Stanford, CA: Hoover Institution, 2005.

Hirsh, S., and J. Killion. *The Learning Educator: A New Era for Professional Learning*. Oxford, OH: National Staff Development Council, 2007.

Killion, J. *Assessing Impact: Evaluating Staff Development*. Second Edition. Oxford, OH: National Staff Development Council, 2007.

Killion, J., L. Munger, P. Roy and P. McMullen. *Training Manual for Assessing Impact: Evaluating Staff Development*. Oxford, OH: National Staff Development Council, 2003.

Knight, J. *Instructional Coaching; A Partnership Approach to Improving Instruction*. Thousand Oaks, CA: Corwin Press, 2007.

Levine, A. *Educating School Leaders*. Washington, D.C. : The Education Schools Project, 2005.

Lieberman, A., and L. Miller. *Teacher Leadership*. San Francisco: Jossey-Bass, 2004.

McLaughlin, M., and J. Talbert. *Building School-Based Teacher Learning Communities*. New York: Teachers College Press, 2006.

Mid-continent Research for Education and Learning (McREL). *The Future of Schooling: Education in American in 2014*. Aurora, CO: McREL, 2005.

National Policy Board for Educational Administration (NPBEA). *Recognizing and Encouraging Exemplary Leadership in America's Schools: A Proposal to Establish a System of Advanced Certification for Administrators*. Arlington, VA: NPBEA, 2001.

Tallerico, M. *Supporting and Sustaining Teachers' Professional Development: A Principal's Guide*. Thousand Oaks, CA: Corwin Press, 2005.

Sanders, N., and J. Simpson. *State Policy Framework to Develop Highly Qualified Educational Administrators*. Washington, D.C. : Council of Chief State School Officers, 2005.

Southern Regional Education Board (SREB). *Schools Can't Wait: Accelerating the Redesign of University Principal Preparation Programs*. Atlanta, GA: SREB, 2006.

Southwest Educational Development Laboratory (SEDL). "Developing a Staff of Learners." *SEDL Letters*. Vol. 19, No. 1. Austin, TX: 2007.

Wenger, E., R. McDermott, W. M. Snyder. *Cultivating Communities of Practice: A Guide to Managing Knowledge*. Boston: Harvard Business Press, 2002.

## Standard Five: Lead Using Knowledge and Data

Baldrige National Quality Program. *Education Criteria for Performance Excellence, 2008*. Washington, D.C. : National Institute of Standards and Technology, U.S. Department of Commerce, 2008.

Keller, B. "Drive On to Improve Evaluation Systems for Teachers." *Education Week*. January 9, 2008 (online), January 16, 2008 (print).

National Board for Professional Teaching Standards Web site: www.nbpts.org.

National Policy Board for Educational Administration (NPBEA): Revised Interstate School Leaders Licensure Consortium Standards (the Educational Leadership Policy Standards) available online at www.npbea.org.

Perlstein, L. *Tested: One American School Struggles to Make the Grade*. New York: Henry Holt, 2007.

Southern Regional Education Board (SREB). *Schools Need Good Leaders Now: State Progress in Building a Learning-Centered School Leadership System*. Atlanta, GA: SREB, 2007.

## Standard Six: Lead Parent, Family and Community Engagement

Annenberg Institute for School Reform. "Engaging Communities." *VUE*. No. 13. Providence, RI: Annenberg Institute for School Reform, 2006.

Boethel, M., A. Averett and C. Jordan. *Thriving Together: Connecting Rural School Improvement and Community Development*. Austin, TX: Southwest Educational Development Laboratory, 2000.

Decker, L. E., and V. Decker. *Home, School, and Community Partnerships*. Lanham, MD: Rowman and Littlefield Publishing Group, 2002.

Ellis, D., and K. Hughes. *Partnerships by Design: Cultivating Effective and Meaningful School-Family-Community Partnerships*. Portland, OR: Northwest Regional Educational Library, 2002.

Epstein, J. L., and K. C. Salinas. "Partnering With Families and Communities." *Schools as Learning Communities*. Vol. 61, No. 8. Alexandria, VA: Association for Supervision and Curriculum Development, 2004.

Rubin, H. *Collaborative Leadership: Developing Effective Partnerships in Communities and Schools*. Thousand Oaks, CA: Corwin Press, 2002.

Peterson, L. *Supporting Parents as Leaders: Stories of Dedication, Determination, and Inspiration*. Boston: Institute for Responsive Education, 2002.

Sanders, M., and A. Harvey. "Beyond the School Walls: A Case Study of Principal Leadership for School-Community Collaboration." *Teachers College Record*. Vol. 104, No. 7. New York: Teachers College, Columbia University, 2002.

## Notes/Reflections